Templar Inferno

Knights of Rebellion

ALSO BY SANFORD HOLST

SWORN IN SECRET
Freemasonry and the Knights Templar

PHOENICIAN SECRETS
Exploring the Ancient Mediterranean

Templar Inferno

Knights of Rebellion

Sanford Holst

SANTORINI
BOOKS

Santorini Publishing
14622 Ventura Boulevard, #800
Los Angeles, California 91403

First Edition
Printing: February 2013

Publisher's Cataloging-In-Publication Data

Holst, Sanford.
    Templar inferno : knights of rebellion /
  Sanford Holst. — 1st ed.

      p. : ill. ; cm.
    Includes bibliographical references and index.
    ISBN: 978-0-9833279-5-0

    1. Templars—History. 2. Freemasons—History. 3. Knights
and knighthood—History. 4. Freemasonry—History. I. Title.

  CR4743 .H65 2013
  271.791/3   2013933288

Contents

Appendix

This is the actual story of people and events that shaped the Knights Templar. Some liberty was taken to express the reaction of individuals to actual events that occurred during their life.

For a well-documented history of these people, places and events, see the author's book *Sworn in Secret*, which contains the detailed facts and sources.

Acknowledgments

Thanks to

John Robinson whose book *Born in Blood* twenty-four years ago inspired me to explore what happened to the Knights Templar.

Dan Brown whose *Da Vinci Code* got us excited again about the mysteries of Templars, Christianity and Masons.

Sir Knight Eduardo, Illustrious Allen, Gudrun, Sheree, Paul, Kristina, Suzanne and each of you who have made a difference in my life.

And of course the Great Architect who is the actual Author of all these things.

Dan Brown's Inferno

$\mathcal{T}$hese are the real people and actual events that make up the surrounding world in which Dan Brown's *Inferno* novel takes place. His hero is once again Robert Langdon, the symbols expert from Harvard University, who travels this time to Florence in Italy. There Dante wrote the original *Inferno*—his exploration of hell and haunting religious issues that still linger today.

So, willing or not, Langdon steps into Dante's world and the world of the Templars. Dante Alighieri lived in Florence and Northern Italy from 1265 until his death in 1321. During that adventurous life he witnessed fateful attacks on the Templars by the Vatican and King Philip of France, which began in 1307. Many of those Templars were burned to death, while others managed to escape to places of concealment. Aware of their torment, Dante felt moved to begin writing his *Inferno*, probing issues of religion and people burning in flames.

The agony of the Templars was not a distant event to Dante. Inquisition officers were sent all over Europe by Pope Clement to support charges of heresy against the Templars. And some of them even came to Florence to conduct trials there. He was keenly aware of those trials but was unable to see them in person because, just like the Templars, he was under the pope's hand—and was banned from his home.

In those days Templars had been living on their estates in Florence, Siena, Pisa and many other parts of Tuscany, so they were an everyday sight. When Clement sent out his order that the Templars be arrested in every Christian land and be held for trial, thirteen knights were seized in Tuscany. They were subjected to painful ordeals in prison after the pope wrote to the bishop of Florence "authorising the use of torture to be more certain to elicit the truth."[1] In other towns public executions were held, with Templars standing on kindling wood and being consumed by fires.

In Dan Brown's *Inferno*, Robert Langdon contends with the things that happened after those events.

The Templars' international financial empire came crashing down around them. It is not known if Templar bankers among the survivors came to work for the Medici family, but when that family started their bank during the 1300s, it became the source of their fabulous wealth and established their dynasty in Florence.

Among the Medici contributions to that city was an intricate system of private passageways for secretive use by the family. The Vasari Corridor alone extended for more than half a mile across Florence. In the windmills of Dan Brown's mind other passageways are discovered and used by the powerful who work in secret to unleash more power.

In history, the aftermath of those attacks on the Templars brought struggles for control as the power of kings and popes fell. And the Renaissance flourished, bringing with it possibilities and perils for the future. We now go on to explore the lives of people intimately involved with the rise, fall and survival of the Templars. It is a fascinating world.

Chapter One

Sir Walter

Before the inferno there were golden days. Sir Walter de Clifton enjoyed those times and the honored life of a Templar knight. He lived on the large Templar estate at Balantrodoch in Scotland, nine miles south of Edinburgh, and his duties were not too difficult. When he went out, his white mantle and its red Templar cross earned signs of respect from passersby as he traveled to the smaller estates owned by his knightly brotherhood in the north.

At those places he gave instructions to Templar servingmen who worked the land, directing the sale of crops for gold and silver coins that would sustain his Order. Upon Sir Walter's return to the manor house at Balantrodoch, he reported to the Templar clerics in their distinctive green robes all that had been learned on his trip. Those well-educated clerics quietly tended to the Templar financial empire that was the envy of all Europe. He then enjoyed the camaraderie of his fellow knights who had traveled in other directions. Beside the bright fire of the manor's large hearth they ate, drank and shared tales of adventure. Then like a bolt of lightning from a clear sky his world was shattered.

Word arrived that on the 13th of October 1307 the soldiers of King Philip had struck suddenly all across France to arrest every

Templar they could find. Their earthly possessions and rich estates had been seized along with them. Walter waited anxiously
for reports from his brethren in that southern land. As the first
French Templar refugees began to arrive at Balantrodoch he was
relieved to learn those knights had been surprisingly elusive.
Roughly a thousand men wore the Templar cross in France at that
time, but only 232 were captured or killed. It was a painful loss of
good men, but it could have been far worse.

Then came word that his Grand Master was weighed down by
chains in a French prison. And the pope—who presided over the
Templar Order—was giving no aid. After a quick meeting in the
manor's chapter room, most of Walter's Scottish brethren did not
wait for further news. They silently disappeared into an "underground" existence. Only Sir Walter and another knight stayed at
Balantrodoch to keep alive the Templar claim on its Scottish lands
and revenue. Without much hope he prayed for the grim reaper's
dark presence to be driven away.

Then Pope Clement yielded to pressure from King Philip and
ordered the arrest of Templars in all the Christian kingdoms. With
that stroke the battle was lost. Sir Walter found himself arrested
and bound over for trial in Edinburgh by the pope's Inquisition.
While he languished in prison, terrifying stories were told by his
inquisitors about the tortures they had used on his compatriots in
France. On the rack his brothers had ropes tied to their hands and
feet, then the bindings were pulled by mechanical devices until
the stretched bones in their wrists and ankles broke loose and
were pulled farther and farther apart, or until confessions of guilt
came tumbling out.

The strappado had also been used. The brother's hands were
tied behind him and the rest of that rope was thrown over a high
ceiling beam. He was pulled up to the ceiling, then released so
that he fell almost to the floor before the taut rope yanked him to a
sudden stop with his arms pulled so far up behind him that he
was in excruciating pain. Then the inquisitors did it again and
again until the confession came. Others were tortured with flames
to sensitive parts of their bodies. All of these things and more
were promised to Walter in the dark cell where he was held. He
was counseled to confess what happened in Templar initiations

Fig. 1   Initiation of a Knight Templar.

and other secret rituals within the Order if he had any hope of saving himself.

Walter endured that torment until the day of his trial, when he was brought before the pope's inquisitors at Holyrood Abbey. He answered their questions as best he could, but did not give the incriminating pieces they sought. What that meant for him in dark cellars later, he did not know. Townspeople and others were likewise called and questioned about what they knew or had heard. The stern inquisitors did their best but could find no blame against him, nor against his Order in Scotland. A bit incredulous, he was set free and allowed to walk out of the courtroom.

Sir Walter rode his horse in haste to the Templar manor house at Balantrodoch, not knowing if some other charges against him might follow. There he wrestled with a difficult decision.

Before his brothers left they had talked of living in secret to remain free of the king's prisons and the inquisitor's fire. They also talked of striking back in covert rebellion against the royal houses and Vatican. Those powers-that-be had already burned some of their brothers to death in a fiery inferno. Others were sure to follow. Now Walter agonized over whether he should join his fugitive companions. But even if he did, what chance did they have of any success?

There was also the thought that if he followed his brothers he could take a wife and start a family, for his days of celibacy as a Templar would come to an end. He could have children. But to protect them from the vicious display of force he had just experienced, perhaps he did not have much choice.

Walter reluctantly took off his white mantle with the red cross. Carefully he laid it on the chapter room table, beside those of his departed brethren. His Templar sword was likewise taken off and placed on top of his mantle, just as the others had done. Gathering his few belongings and a nondescript cloak, Walter went downstairs, closed the large front door behind him and locked it for the last time.

For reasons of safety, his brothers had not told him where they were hidden, so he had been able to answer honestly at his trial that he knew not where they were. But he knew where they would come to find him. So he mounted his horse, rode under the stone archway at the manor's gatehouse, and followed a dirt road that soon took him off the Templar estate. That world was behind him now, and a new world lay ahead.

Like his brothers, Sir Walter knew the strength of Templar knighthood had grown from roots that went deep into antiquity, even to Solomon's Temple. Now he had to find his brothers and reach back to the source of that strength once more.

King Hiram

On a hill high above Jerusalem the Temple of Solomon rested in regal splendor. A wonder in its day, this house of God evoked such emotions that its name and image endured for three thousand years. Precious to the Jewish people, it gained an additional aura when Jesus entered that sacred place and discussed beliefs with the temple priests. In time the mount upon which it stood would become the home of the Knights Templar, who then immersed themselves in the glory and mysteries of this Temple.

Yet who crafted those masonry walls of pale stone, set the massive cedar beams of its roof, raised two mighty pillars of brass at the temple entrance and covered almost all of its interior in gold leaf? The sacred books of Judaism that became the Old Testament of the Bible told us the Hebrew people had never built a temple before. So they called upon King Hiram whose Phoenician people lived in Lebanon just north of Israel.

The Phoenicians had built many temples in their cities along the coast from Tyre to Byblos. Their king had also given a similar gift to Solomon's father, for it was written, "And Hiram king of Tyre sent messengers to David, and cedar trees, and carpenters, and masons; and they built David a house".[2]

Hiram was only nineteen years of age when this heavy crown of Tyre was placed upon his head. Even so, he shouldered the burden of building this peace offering to David, and that elegant palace was raised on the southern slope of Mount Moriah in Jerusalem.

Yet that was not his only care, for he kept the rest of his masons busy at home. His city of Tyre rested on an island half a mile from the Lebanese coast. This was an ideal place for his sea-going people, but the small size of the island limited what his people could do there—and young Hiram dreamed of greater things. So he summoned his masons and set them to work building seawalls and landfill to expand his island to 40 acres. The small eastern harbor was greatly expanded, and as was the second harbor in the west.

Soon he had a much larger fleet of ships sailing from these harbors to foreign lands. So he began to transform those distant places as well. Many of the small Phoenician outposts around the Mediterranean now became actual colonies with their own stone harbors and fine buildings. And with these changes his people's small trade routes became highways across the seas. In recognition of this stunning rise in fortunes, the lesser kings of other Phoenician cities began deferring to him as the leader of their people. He had full authority to deal with the kings of Israel or any other land and, though he could not know it, would in time be regarded as one of the greatest of the Phoenician kings.

His neighbor King David passed away in the year 970 BC, and David's son Solomon came to sit on the throne in Jerusalem. It soon became evident that this new king of Israel had a grand dream of his own.

> And Solomon sent to Hiram, saying, "Thou knowest how that David my father could not build an house unto the name of the LORD his God for the wars which were about him on every side, until the LORD put them under the soles of his feet. But now the LORD my God hath given me rest on every side, so that there is neither adversary nor evil occurrent. And, behold, I purpose to build an house unto the name of the LORD

my God, as the LORD spake unto David my father, say-
ing, Thy son, whom I will set upon thy throne in thy
room, he shall build an house unto my name. Now
therefore command thou that they hew me cedar trees
out of Lebanon....

1 Kings 5:2-6

King Hiram delivered all the cedar, masons and artisans Solomon required, and also provided him with a master mason who
came to be known as Hiram Abiff. For seven years they labored to
transform rough stones, molten brass, huge cedar logs and bars of
gold into an awe-inspiring place of worship. This miraculous
temple was also said to contain a crypt filled with valuable objects
and writings of great power. Solomon and his people joyfully and
publicly celebrated this worthy symbol of their dedication to God.
But Hiram spoke not at all about what his people had put into the
temple, and how it might be used.

It was not unusual that Hiram chose to do this, for his people
had always been exceptionally secretive, even in their earliest
days. He knew their first fame and fortune in those days came
from harvesting the towering and long-lasting cedars of Lebanon
from the Lebanon Mountains which ran the length of their small
country. This land is still called Lebanon to the present day. Yet it
is what his Phoenician people did with that bounty that made
them unique and memorable. They fashioned the great cedar logs
into large ships capable of traveling long distances across the open
sea with large cargoes. And with that they became the great sea
traders of antiquity.

They launched that enterprise by bringing beams of cedar
wood to Egypt in 3200 BC. Their rich trade with that land continued during most of the dynasties that followed. That enabled his
people's first, small fishing village of Byblos to grow into a rich
city with massive walls all around it, and beautiful civic buildings
within. His prosperous Phoenician forebears then overflowed
southward to found cities at Sidon and Tyre, and northward to
the island of Arwad. Their large cedar boats carried rich fabrics
and gold from Egypt, wine and olive oil from the Greek isles, and
mountains of copper from Cyprus.

Their tremendously lucrative trade with Egypt was still active in the years around 2550 BC when the Great Pyramid was built at Giza. The Egyptians left ample evidence of this, for they were not bound by the same strict rule of secrecy as the Phoenicians. This took the form of two cedar-of-Lebanon boats buried beside the pyramid as part of the funerary ceremonies for the fallen king. One of those cedar boats can still be seen there today.

From the time of the pyramid also came the all-seeing eye, which was believed to be a powerful talisman of protection. Hiram knew for certain that the all-seeing eye had long been painted on the prow of Phoenician boats to protect them on their journeys, and had heard the Egyptians did the same. His own Phoenician ships marked with the all-seeing eye traveled the length of the Mediterranean and out to the Atlantic coast of Europe, having particularly long-standing relationships with Malta and Portugal. Marking boats in this manner was a tradition continued forever after in those places. The combined symbol of Great Pyramid and all-seeing eye was well known to his people.

Hiram's forebears had greatly improved their skill with masonry during the years they observed the building of the Great Pyramid. They then practiced this craft often, becoming highly skilled in the construction of stone harbors, walls and buildings. He valued these craftsmen highly for the work they did expanding his city of Tyre, and was confident enough to have these men work on Solomon's Temple.

His people's extraordinarily strict secrecy likewise dated back to those early trading days. They were especially careful to protect their trade routes so that others could not take some of their rich trade. The ancient historian Strabo[3] told of a Phoenician captain who saw he was being followed by a foreign ship and purposefully guided both vessels onto the rocks so that the secret route would not be discovered. Hiram expected the same of his own captains.

These extreme measures were also applied to Phoenician writings. Many people in Hiram's society were prolific writers, particularly the sea traders who traveled across the Mediterranean. Because of those traveling emissaries, Hiram knew the Phoenician alphabet was being used in many foreign lands and then adapted

Fig. 2   Cedar boat at the Great Pyramid

to local needs. In later years the Greek historian Herodotus witnessed the creation of the Greek alphabet drawn from the Phoenician one.

Hiram carefully continued the Phoenician custom of absolute secrecy with regard to his people's affairs. It became his duty, as it was for the Phoenician leaders who went before him, to make sure none of their writings or books ever fell in to the hands of outsiders.

The other people of his day were well aware of this Phoenician custom, and rumors abounded that secret hiding places were built into or under Solomon's Temple. Into these places would have been put the Ark of the Covenant, the stone tablets of Moses, sacred and occult Jewish writings such as Kabbalah, and golden objects of immense value.

As it turns out, a secret hiding place actually existed. Almost three thousand years after Hiram's day, I was able to go into that crypt under the site of Solomon's Temple. The path there was indicated by a man known as the Pilgrim of Bordeaux who wrote about his visit to Temple Mount in 333 AD. He reported that Jewish visitors still came and anointed the "perforated rock" opening, while wailing and rending their garments. On my own pilgrimage there in 1997 I went into that crypt and looked up through the opening to where the Holy of Holies would have been. Unfortunately the crypt itself now contained so much manmade material that finding traces of things left behind was almost impossible. Since legends tell us the Knights Templar explored diligently and took away anything still secreted there in 1119 AD, the likelihood of finding much more than chips of stone or fragments of parchment at this point is somewhat remote.

Hiram's decision to help Solomon build a temple to God as worshiped by the Jewish people was not a personal decision made on the spur of the moment. It reflected a deeply-ingrained practice of religious tolerance among his people. Even in his own day he could visit the magnificent temple of Our Lady in Byblos, the first Phoenician city. There visitors were allowed and encouraged to call this feminine deity by whatever name they were most comfortable. Egyptian visitors called her Hathor, the goddess most similar to Our Lady in the Egyptian pantheon. Canaanite visitors

Fig. 3 The pierced rock—the round opening to the crypt below Solomon's Temple—is shown at upper left in this view from above

from other cities could, and did, call her Astarte. Greeks would later call her Aphrodite, and the Romans knew her as Venus. All these names were acceptable to his people without hesitation. Prominently displayed in Byblos were gifts from foreign dignitaries addressed to one or more of these names.

To make this worship possible, it was the firm Phoenician practice to allow no graven image of a deity in their temples. Instead they used a simple stone marker to identify the sacred place where prayers could be offered. This stone had a square base and tapered as it went higher, being capped with a small pyramid. They called this marker a *maṣṣebah*. The same shape was used by the Egyptians on a larger scale and was called an obelisk. Since the shape and appearance of the *maṣṣebah* was the same for all deities, every worshiper could pray in the temple with equal comfort.

Hiram knew this was not so much an altruistic or enlightened practice as it was an exceedingly practical one. A leading cause of war at that time was fighting over differences in religion. His people were a small society and by no means a military match for the nations around them. So this threat to their existence was removed by standing in prayer beside others, even if their beliefs were different. There seemed to be considerable value in this practice, because his Phoenician people survived for many centuries while those around them perished one by one.

This of course had deeply affected his decision on Solomon's Temple. When the Hebrew king asked for help in building a temple to God as worshipped by the Jewish people, Hiram acted without hesitation. He accepted the offer and sent his best masons. The temple took shape in stone, cedar, brass and gold, standing in radiant sunlight on its hill above Jerusalem.

Of course there was no way he could know that this ancient temple and his Phoenician people were to be of great value to the Templars who would one day guard the city of Tyre and live in Jerusalem on the temple's sacred ground.

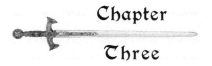
Mary and Helena

Jesus of Nazareth was still a boy when he first came to the Temple of Solomon. Almost a thousand years had passed since King Hiram sent masons to work on this revered place of worship, and it had been much rebuilt so that it still inspired awe in those fortunate enough to step within. Yet Jesus seemed completely at ease on this hallowed ground, and engaged the surprised temple priests in discussions with a seriousness beyond his years. Later, Jesus returned as a grown man to drive moneychangers from this house of God. He also walked the Holy Land while preaching, and spoke words that inspired twelve devoted disciples as well as a young woman named Mary Magdalene.

Mary was attracted to Jesus, and the feeling seemed to be returned. She joined him at what witnesses attested to be the performing of miracles. And together they began to build a life. Yet if they were ever wed she kept that a secret. Some said she bore his child and started a royal bloodline. But if further proof exists for such a legacy, it still needs to be brought forward and has not yet come to light. Whatever thoughts she had for their life together were unfortunately shattered when Jesus was compelled to walk up Golgotha Hill in Jerusalem carrying a cross. He was then crucified in front of her. When she went in mourning three days later to the nearby gravesite, there was no body there to be found.

All these things had a profound effect on her and on the thousands of followers who had heard the words of Jesus. His teachings of course gave rise to Christianity, and the twelve apostles set out in all directions to carry this message to the people of foreign lands.

Conflicting accounts exist about whether Mary suffered persecution in her later years, but there is no doubt that many members of this new religion were persecuted and killed by followers of older beliefs. Ruthless treatment of captured Christians was etched into people's minds by images of Nero throwing helpless Christians to lions and other animals in Roman arenas. During those perilous times Christians met cautiously in hidden places such as the underground catacombs of Rome. They were essentially a secret society.

It is said that they used the symbol of a fish as their recognition sign, since Christ had told his disciples "I will make you fishers of men." This simple symbol could be scratched on the wall of a building being used for a religious meeting so followers would know where to go. Then it could just as easily be erased afterwards. This also served as a recognition sign among strangers, especially when traveling. One person would draw a single arc on the ground. If the other person drew a second arc to complete the fish symbol, they each knew they had met a fellow member of this

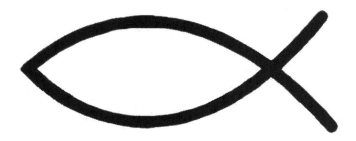

Fig. 4 Fish symbol of the Christian secret society

select group. The symbol is still popularly used today as a sign of Christianity.

That makes it particularly strange that the Catholic Church and many other Christian denominations have taken such strong stands against secret societies. Perhaps it is because they know from personal experience how powerful these societies can become.

The Roman empress Helena was born of humble origins about two hundred years later near Byzantium, the city that would soon be re-named Constantinople in honor of her son, Emperor Constantine the Great. Her marriage to a Roman officer seemed secure and her son was nearly seventeen years of age, so she was shocked when the officer abruptly divorced her. She found consolation in Christianity. He callously remarried and moved west to Europe where he gained the title of Caesar, a position just below the emperor. There he called for his son to join him.

Helena remained near Byzantium but followed the struggles of young Constantine. He survived the risks of war and proved himself an able commander on the battlefield. Upon her ex-husband's death, the title of Caesar came to Constantine and a better day seemed possible. But her son then had to fight a series of battles over who would succeed the old emperor, and several times found himself in dire situations where all could be lost. At those extreme moments he called upon the faith of his mother and marked the sign of Christ on the shields of his men. Each time he prevailed. When at last he succeeded and came home to Byzantium as emperor in 324 AD, Helena joined him in the imperial court.

From that moment all persecutions against Christians in the Roman empire were lifted. As a result the number of Christians began to multiply and their form of worship eventually became dominant from the Middle East all the way to Britain and Ireland.

Helena's favorite cause was also the subject of the Council of Nicea which was held at this town near Constantinople to bring order to the different sects that had sprung up among early Christians. The assembled bishops and representatives from those sects debated articles of faith and set the stage for a later council that decided which gospels should be included in the Bible and which

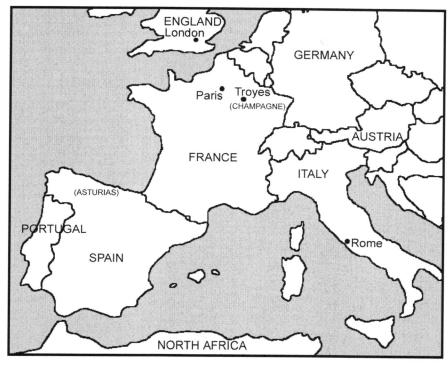

Fig. 5 Map of Europe

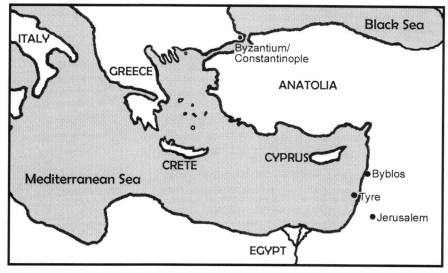

Fig. 6 Map of the Eastern Mediterranean

should be excluded. The result of their decisions was essentially the Christianity we know today.

Even then she was not finished influencing the course of this young religion. The memory of Jesus was poorly maintained and little visible in the Holy Land, so she took it upon herself to reverse those years of neglect. She led a major expedition to Jerusalem and the surrounding lands where Jesus had worked miracles, preached and suffered before the crucifixion. With great diligence she found those places, some fully covered over or concealed, and in the emperor's name she built churches at those sites.

The most famous of these venerated places was the site where Jesus was believed to have been buried and then arose on the third day. Here she removed many layers of rubble to discover the gravesite and pieces of wood that were thought to be parts of the cross upon which Jesus had hung. She built the magnificent Church of the Holy Sepulcher there with its prominent round tower. This church would become one of the cornerstones of the Crusades and an important icon to the Knights Templar.

As Helena raised the churches at these special places across the Holy Land she unknowingly enticed large waves of pilgrims to begin traveling there from all over the Christian world.

Then came Muhammad. In Saudi Arabia he called the Arab people to his impassioned teachings that became known as Islam. When he died in 632 AD it set off a frenzy of conquest that quickly spread north to the Caucasus Mountains, east to Iran, and west across North Africa as far as Morocco. It then crossed the Strait of Gibraltar and consumed Spain and Portugal. This changed the lives of many people. And yet it is true that some Christians survived in this vast array of newly converted lands. In Lebanon about half the country remained Christian, and those people fiercely defended their enclaves in the Lebanon Mountains.

The fighting in Europe continued when Muslim armies poured forth from their base in Spain and pierced the western side of France. There they were confronted by Charles Martel who finally stopped their advance near the city of Poitiers. Charles also started a great line of French kings which included his grandson, Charlemagne.

Only twenty-eight years of age when he became king, Charlemagne launched a series of changes that gave rise to knighthood, transformed Europe, and brought the known world a step closer to the Crusades. A great leader of men, he set out on military campaigns that expanded his patrimony eastward to include most of Germany and Austria. He led his troops southward to bring in Italy as far as the city of Rome, and westward past the Pyrenees to take and hold Barcelona. But all of this was not easy, and he lost his brother during these years.

Charlemagne also did more than conquer. He established Christianity and the power of the pope across Europe, bringing them to a level never before seen or imagined. His successful campaigns had brought Christianity to many new lands, and he established it further by appointing clergy to major roles in administering his empire. Since the clergy were the only literate people at that time, they were the writers of history and warmly responded to his support by naming him Charles the Great, which in its Latin form has come down to us as Charlemagne.

Those campaigns had another benefit as well, because by conquering Northern Italy and the lands around Rome, he freed the pope from harassment by local kings. In gratitude, Pope Leo III conferred an extraordinary gift upon Charlemagne, crowning him Emperor of the Romans in 800 AD. This act transformed the king's vast collection of conquered lands into the Holy Roman Empire. To be fair, this revived only the *Western* Roman Empire, since the Roman empire in the East had continued without interruption—known as the Byzantine Empire—with its emperor still residing in Constantinople.

In return for this crown, Charlemagne unwittingly gave the pope something of incredible value. It was essentially a grant of power and authority over church and state.

After the crucifixion of Jesus, the twelve apostles had served as bishops, establishing local priests and acting together to lead the church. Peter had been the senior among them, and settled in Rome. So the bishop of Rome continued to be a leading voice among the Christian bishops, but had no commanding authority over them. In fact, the bishops of Antioch, Jerusalem and Alexandria were sometimes considered more powerful. The honorary title of pope only allowed the Roman bishop to be heard over the many differing voices within the church.

All of that changed when Charlemagne allowed Pope Leo III to place oil on his forehead and declare him the Holy Roman Emperor. That act established the precedent and practice that no man could become emperor unless anointed or blessed by the pope. This concept rapidly expanded to give the pope religious authority over all Christian kings and over the Catholic Church. That incredible power was jealously guarded by successive popes who sought to strengthen it and exercise it whenever possible.

Charlemagne's strong rule across much of Europe was also credited with giving rise to knighthood. This practice grew out of the general state of warfare that existed across Europe's countless local lands and fiefdoms. Among these many confrontations, the deeds of the legendary officers of Charlemagne stood out. Those men were mounted soldiers who took to the field heavily armed and played major roles in his victories. When not engaged in war, they also tried to maintain some semblance of peace. These early knights soon became a fixture throughout Europe. They embodied the leading image of the Middle Ages, arrayed in shining armor, seated upon a great warhorse, and charging across bloody battlefields in an age when kings fought kings for conquests.

One of the most popular fields across which these knights fought belonged to the neighboring kingdom of Asturias in Northern Spain. It had the distinction of being the last Christian enclave in the Iberian peninsula, and had successfully held out against the Muslim forces. From the fields of Asturias came the *Reconquista*, the slow and difficult reconquering of the lands of Spain and Portugal. Those clashes within the Iberian peninsula would continue until the 1400s, with the Templars playing a significant role. But that was in the future.

In its early years, the powerful message of the *Reconquista* to all Europeans was that the fight between Christian and Muslim armies was not a distant, overseas problem. It was one that existed on their own doorstep. And the slow but sure Christian successes in Spain and Portugal gave a widespread sense of elation. It instilled in Europeans the firm belief that embarking on Crusades to the Holy Land was a contest Christians would win.

Count Hugh de Champagne

Hugh de Payens was the ideal choice for first Grand Master of
the Knights Templar. Born into a small but well-established aristocratic family in France during 1070 AD, he became a young lord
upon the passing of his father. Hugh's fertile estate seventy miles
southeast of Paris was part of the influential province of Champagne, a region that produced the sparkling beverage of the same
name.

Since his manor house rested only seven miles from Champagne's capital city of Troyes, he was soon drawn into the great
events changing the face of France. One of those occurred when
Hugh was twenty-three: a young man four years his junior became the Count of Champagne. Although he was a vassal of the
new Count, who was also named Hugh, de Payens seemed to be
admired by the younger man. That was an extremely useful
friendship, for Count Hugh de Champagne ruled one of the largest provinces in France and stepped into its society at a level just
below the king.

De Payens was also fascinated by the storm clouds of the Crusades that were beginning to form. A call for Holy War came from
the Byzantine Christian emperor in Constantinople, who ruled

over the remnants of the Eastern Roman Empire. Seljuk Turks had overrun his southern lands, which would come to be known as Turkey. Then they continued south and captured Jerusalem. These invaders brought with them a more aggressive and stringent form if Islam, so it was not only the emperor who suffered but the local churches and Christian pilgrims as well. In Rome, Pope Urban II found the emperor's pleas especially appealing because it meant unifying all Christians in Europe on a mission with the pope as its spiritual leader. This passion for a Crusade quickly spread across the Christian lands. Hugh de Payens was among those caught up in the fervor and joined the First Crusade. He set out for the Holy Land in 1096 alongside many other knights of Europe.

On that pilgrimage he endured three grueling years of battles fought by this patched-together collection of Western armies, and experienced their triumphant surge over the walls of Jerusalem. Battered and weary, most of his fellow soldiers were satisfied to declare a great victory and return home. That left him among the few fighting men who had to hold the Holy Land against the surrounding hostile bands of warriors.

Meanwhile in France, Count Hugh de Champagne barely survived an assassination attempt on his life. This shocking reminder of his mortality caused him to consider a more religious life. It also made him reflect on the years he spent with Hugh de Payens, who was always four years older than himself, and always seemed more mature and experienced. So he made a trip to the spiritual center of that age, the Holy Land, and became reunited with his friend.

In that special place Count Hugh lived the demanding but rewarding life of a knight amid the dangers of the countryside. He also renewed his relationship with Baldwin of Boulogne, the king of Jerusalem, whose family ruled the province north of his own in France. Reinvigorated, Count Hugh returned to Europe in 1107, bringing along his friend de Payens.

In Champagne once more, Count Hugh became actively involved in supporting the work of Cistercian monks. This reformed branch of the black-robed Benedictine Order distinguished itself

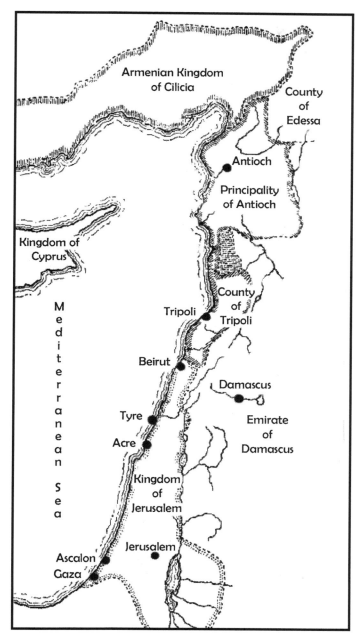

Fig. 7   Map of the Holy Land during the Crusades

by choosing white robes to identify their Cistercian Order. Count Hugh made good on his pledge to be more involved with the religious side of life by making a generous grant of lands to a young Cistercian monk named Bernard. This enabled the monk to establish a monastery at Clairvaux in France, just east of Troyes. And in time the newly-made abbot became known as Saint Bernard. A gifted man, Saint Bernard never forgot the debt he owed to his benefactor and accordingly became of great service to the Knights Templar.

In 1114 Hugh de Payens returned to the Holy Land. While looking for ways to be of greater service, he became aware of a group of local brothers in Jerusalem who provided hospital care for sick and weary pilgrims. These men were the Hospitallers.

Capture of the Holy Land had thrown open the door to a large influx of pilgrims from Europe and the Byzantine Empire. Yet the long and arduous pilgrimage took a severe toll on many whose spirits were stronger than their bodies. To their aid came this obscure group of Benedictine monks attached to the monastery of Saint John, who provided shelter and medical care for the afflicted. An able man named Gerard Thom became provost of this casual group and organized them into a formal religious order known as Hospitallers. Under his guidance the new order began to receive rich grants of property to support its much-needed work. The highest validation of their efforts came in 1113, when Pope Paschal II formally recognized them as the Order of Saint John of Jerusalem. The official garb granted to them was the black robe of the Benedictines, but with a white cross added. They had no military role at that time. They simply served as monks providing shelter and medical care.

Hugh was also aware of the need for an order of knights in the Holy Land, made abundantly clear by the dire plight of Christian pilgrims. The few remaining knights could barely defend major cities such as Jerusalem, Jaffa, Beirut and Antioch, which left the rest of the land exposed. Although Islamic leaders were unable to raise a sufficient force to regain those cities, they could—and did—put countless small raiding parties on the highways and dirt roads of the Holy Land.

A particularly bloody massacre of pilgrims in 1119 finally caused de Payens to gather eight other knights to stand with him and form the Knights Templar. When he met with King Baldwin to tell of the solemn obligation he and the other men had taken, the monarch was overjoyed. In gratitude he gave Sir Hugh and his new order of knights a wing of the royal palace on Temple Mount for their residence and meeting place. This building previously served as Al Aqsa Mosque and had a great hall with many adjoining rooms. Since their new headquarters stood on the mount once graced by the Temple of Solomon, Hugh's knights felt moved to call themselves Knights of the Temple.

Their official name would later be confirmed by the pope as *Pauperes commilitones Christi Templique Solomonici,* or the Poor Fellow-Soldiers of Christ and the Temple of Solomon. The reference to poverty reflected other vows taken by Hugh and his knights, in addition to protecting pilgrims. They swore to act in a more holy manner than many of their rough-hewn fellow Crusaders, and took vows of poverty, chastity, and obedience. By these vows, the Knights Templar assumed the lives of monks, just as one might find in an abbey or monastery. But instead of remaining isolated behind abbey walls their mission required them to be active in the world with sword in hand, fighting against any who attacked Christians in the Holy Land.

It was no coincidence that all of these first Templars lived in or near Sir Hugh's home province of Champagne before they came to the Holy Land. They were a close group of men whom de Payens and Count Hugh of Champagne had come to know well, and in whom they put complete trust.

Grand Master Hugh and his Templars gradually adopted a uniform similar to the white robes of the Cistercian monks, but marked by a distinctive red cross. Though other forms of dress would later be added within their Order, this was the famous image by which they came to be known on the battlefield and in people's imaginations around the world.

Hugh soon discovered that all knights returning to Europe from the Holy Land were accorded some measure of respect, but those who also took these vows of poverty, chastity, and obedience to God were raised to a higher level. These vows did not allow him or his men to enrich themselves personally. Nor could they establish a dynasty for their heirs, as others had done across the continent. Instead the Templars were only allowed to use their formidable power in the service of pilgrims and God. This endeared them to lords and commons alike.

Taking the field at the head of his men, Sir Hugh quickly began to have some effect on battles in the Holy Land. And if imitation is the sincerest form of flattery, then the Hospitallers now paid the Templars the ultimate compliment. When the founder of the Hospitallers, Gerard Thom, died in 1120, this order of monks elected Raymond du Puy to lead them. Being a knight himself, and having seen the honors heaped upon the Knights Templar when they were formed the previous year, du Puy resolved to add a knightly dimension to his own monastic order. He actively recruited a number of knights and formed a separate group alongside the monks who still provided shelter and care for pilgrims. These then took to the battlefields of the Holy Land with their knightly armor covered by distinctive black robes marked with a white cross. They served alongside—and sometimes in competition with—the Knights Templar, whose shining armor was covered by white robes and a bright red cross.

As de Payens established his Templars in their knightly duties another benefit came his way courtesy of Baldwin II. The king decided to move to the Tower of David in the western part of the city, leaving the Templars in sole possession of the building they knew as Solomon's Temple. This change caused the Grand Master to "secure the perimeter" by intensely searching the buildings and passageways on or under Temple Mount. In the course of this work the Templars were said to have acquired secrets and powers that enabled them to quickly rise to a position of tremendous authority and wealth in Europe and the East.

These secrets and powers were attributed to discoveries involving Solomon's Temple, and covered a wide range. A Holy Grail or cup was said to have held the blood of Jesus and retained tremendous powers. The Ark of the Covenant, with or without the stone tablets containing the ten commandments, was likewise believed to have great power.

One of the secrets suggested in the book *Holy Blood, Holy Grail* in 1982 and made popular by *The Da Vinci Code* was that the Templars discovered and protected the bloodline of Jesus, who was thought to have fathered a child by Mary Magdalene. This reportedly began a dynasty of secret descendants of Jesus, with serious repercussions for the Catholic Church.

Other discoveries were said to be secret manuscripts such as Kabbalah and other Hebrew religious writings which contained the answers to great mysteries. These included encrypted number systems and secret messages that could be interpreted from the Bible, and which transmitted divine power.

All of these things had their believers and advocates, and in some cases the arguments presented on their behalf were quite compelling.

Yet it is also certain that in addition to whatever relics and documents were found under the mount, Sir Hugh obtained something else in connection with Solomon's Temple that proved to be of tremendous value. He found the descendants of the Phoenicians who had helped to build the temple.

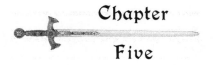

Sir Hugh de Payens

When the Crusaders swept north from Jerusalem into Lebanon and sacked the Muslim coastal cities, Sir Hugh was among them. That campaign changed everything for the Lebanese Christians. They had lived in those coastal cities before being pushed out by the Arab Conquest and forced to take refuge in the Lebanon Mountains. Now he watched them pour down from the hills into those cities again, where they happily rebuilt their churches and communities. Many also earned a good living providing whatever services and supplies were needed by the Crusaders. And they became crucial to Hugh's newly-formed Templars.

We usually think of the Templars as knights on horseback who rode off to battle, and indeed many of them were. Yet the Templars were also far more complex than that. At their height, they had 900 knights and 6300 support people in their Order. This ratio was maintained to greater or lesser degree throughout the life of their brotherhood. When Hugh first formed the Templars in Jerusalem, he began to fill those support positions with the few members of his personal staff who had not returned to Europe. But as his new Order added more knights he had to recruit many more servingmen to support them. About ten years after his knightly brotherhood began he had thirty knights and roughly 200 serv-ingmen. Some of the people he recruited had a major impact on the Templars.

To be sure, there were many traditional workmen among these supporting brothers. Some were assigned to direct battle-related duties while others performed myriad non-military tasks. They acquired armor and horses, procured and prepared the daily food, maintained the living quarters and performed many other needed services. Some were assigned to work on the estates donated to the Templars, raising buildings or laboring to produce the crops that augmented the knights' revenue. These servingmen or ser-geants as they were sometimes called, were required to wear sim-ple black or brown robes surmounted by the red Templar cross.

Yet Sir Hugh also recruited people with special skills to serve as clerical brothers. These men formed a separate group within the Order and were assigned unique and intriguing responsibili-ties. They were literate, skilled in business affairs, and eventually became recognized by their distinct appearance and influence.

The early mark distinguishing these clerical brothers was their ability to read and write. In those early days, literacy and further education were mainly reserved for priests and other clerics. Eu-rope's Medieval Dark Age was dimly lit by a few religious scribes who made copies of ancient writings by Greek, Roman and other authors. Their work preserved those insights and teachings at a time when a good sword was usually regarded as more important than a good book. Europeans had only slowly begun to emerge from that rustic state by the time of the Crusades. Some members of nobility were taught the rudiments of reading, but generally the task of writing and recording was left to religious clerics retained for that purpose.

Originally the word *cleric* meant a person who was ordained into the priesthood. However it descended in common usage to the word *clerk*, which meant a person who could read, write, and keep records. The white-clad Knights Templar from noble fami-lies—following the custom of their peers—left the writing and record-keeping to their literate clerks.

This created a problem. In those early days the church leaders did not allow Sir Hugh to have ordained clerics in his new Order.

He was limited to lay brothers only. This made him dependent on outside clerics, and exposed all of his men's private affairs, written communications and financial dealings to others. In sharp contrast to this, he was a man who preferred to keep his affairs private, as shown by the intense secrecy with which he and his successors shielded their actions. So it is easy to imagine how being forced to depend on outsiders must have galled him.

The solution proved to be a simple one. Sir Hugh just ignored this restriction and privately cultivated his own group of literate brothers. In the meantime, he lobbied heavily to have the restriction lifted. To keep these brothers concealed he gave them the title of chaplain, and charged them with reading prayers and Bible verses to the knights and servingmen. Twenty years after his Order was founded, Hugh finally won the pope's permission to have ordained clerics among the Templars. With that dispensation, the third suborder of Knights Templar—after the knights and servingmen—was born. These brothers were known as the clerics or "green robes"

> Third came the clerics—priests who acted as chaplains to the order and, because they were the only group of the three with any claim to literacy, frequently acted as scribes and record keepers and were responsible for other duties of a nonmilitary character. The clerics also wore the Templar cross, on a green mantle. The clerics wore gloves at all times, to keep their hands clean for "when they touch God" in serving mass. The clerics were clean-shaven, according to the custom of the time, while the knights were required to keep their hair cut short but to let their beards grow.[4]

In recruiting the large number of servingmen and clerics needed to support his knights, Sir Hugh discovered there were too few Europeans left in the Holy Land after the capture of Jerusalem. Fortunately there was a source of help.

Ever since he had arrived with the Crusaders, Hugh had seen that the Lebanese Christians were willing and able to provide many of the services his men needed. So now he began to take some of them into his new Templar Order. They were dressed in black or brown robes with the red Templar cross, just like the other men, and a significant number of them soon showed they were more than common laborers.

Much like their Phoenician ancestors, these Lebanese people were well-known for their remarkable business skills. Sir Hugh had seen how daunting a task it was for Europeans to forage for food and other supplies in the Middle East. Yet it was a normal day's work for those raised in this land. Local Christians caused the needed goods to flow and were able to perform many of the labors required of servingmen in the Order. It was a match made in heaven. Nor were they limited to handling household matters.

Part of Hugh's duties as Templar Grand Master was to rebuild the walls his men had destroyed while capturing cities in the Holy Land. He also needed to add strong castles for use in battles that were certain to come. In short, he needed skilled masons.

So it was with great relief that he discovered these Lebanese people were heirs to the masonry tradition which had risen to great heights with the building of Solomon's Temple and other projects. Crafting perfectly-cut stones was a Phoenician hallmark and they had used it to create stone harbors, walls and buildings at their many cities and colonies around the Mediterranean. Now those abilities were put to use on behalf of the Templars—at Tyre and many other cities—to build the fortifications that were needed. The masons among the Lebanese Christians proved to be of great value.

Europeans had likewise refined their stoneworking skills since the days Roman builders introduced aqueducts, massive walls, fortresses and then churches in that northern land. The merging of European and Phoenician traditions in the Holy Land produced outstanding results. Some of the Templar buildings raised by his masons still stand on Temple Mount, including the three massive central arches leading into the Grand Master's main hall. Given the life-or-death need for fortifications in the Holy Land, the ability of Lebanese Christians to provide masons was an essential contribution.

Sir Hugh found that hiring local Christians in Lebanon had another benefit as well. The early Phoenicians had been highly

Fig. 8   Templar arches still stand on Temple Mount

literate people who brought their alphabet to many other lands. He needed people who could keep the Order's records, write contracts for supplies, and handle correspondence between the Holy Land and Europe, and the Lebanese Christians turned out to be better able to perform these tasks than the knights themselves.

His special interest in the Lebanese people, and the continued interest of his successors, was manifested many times. After the Lebanese city of Tripoli was captured by the Crusaders it was turned over to the Templars for protection. Beirut also became a Crusader town, and in time its protection was transferred to the Templars. At Sidon, the Crusader Castle-by-the-Sea was built in a strategic position beside the harbor, and on a nearby hillside the fortress of St. Louis was raised. The Templars purchased the rights to hold Sidon, consolidating their control of Lebanese lands. Farther inland, they assumed the rights to the castle of Beaufort. After the city of Tyre finally fell into Christian hands in 1124, Hugh gained for his Templars a share in its control as well.

The similarity between duties of the green-robed brothers among the Knights Templar and services provided by Lebanese Christians was not a coincidence. For Sir Hugh to recruit literate people with business talents from Europe would have been inordinately expensive. And such people would still have had to learn the local Arabic language. Instead he took the easy way out and drew upon local Christians in Lebanon for these clerical services.

Trust-building between his Western troops and the local Lebanese was significantly aided by the fact that they were both Christians, and were beset by ardent Muslim opponents on all sides.

This was taken further by the vows and obligations required of new members in the Templar Order. These oaths were sworn by all the brothers, from highest to lowest, drawing them closer together. The passing years would show these vows were kept, even in life-and-death situations. Hugh's Templars were notoriously firm about living up to their obligations. They did not leave a wounded brother upon the field, nor retreat individually while the battle was being fought. They were known for fighting to the death, rather than break the vow made to their brothers. The bond of brotherhood among all these Templars became unshakable.

Saint Bernard

In the year 1125 the Count Hugh of Champagne did a most re-markable thing. For many years he had been quietly active in the rise of the Knights Templar, but now he chose to make his in-volvement more explicit. Handing over the hereditary rights of Champagne to his nephew, he came to the Holy Land and took the vows of the Templar Order, placing his hands in those of his lifelong friend, the Grand Master. By doing so Hugh stepped out of the public spotlight. Yet he redoubled his efforts behind the scenes during this critical moment for the young Templars. Famil-iar with the affairs of Europe, the newly-dubbed knight knew that to be more than a minor cult in Jerusalem, the small brotherhood in which he now lived had to obtain the pope's formal approval and blessing. The brothers also needed ongoing financial support from the nobility of Europe.

According to popular legend, King Baldwin II of Jerusalem de-cided one day in 1126 to send a request to the influential Saint Bernard, Abbot of Clairvaux, asking the abbot to seek the pope's blessing for the Knights Templar. Bernard was said to have ac-cepted this mission for no particular reason and things progressed from there. The reality, of course, was somewhat different. The

saintly Bernard had received the lands for his monastery at Clairvaux from the hands of Count Hugh, and owed him a profound
debt of gratitude. Bernard made this clear in his letter written to
the Count when Hugh left France to become a Templar. It was
never in doubt that Bernard would be a passionate advocate for
the Templars when needed. The request for his support clearly
came from the former Count via Grand Master de Payens, who
arranged for King Baldwin II to sign the letter so it would have
more weight when Saint Bernard presented it to the pope. Bernard
promptly obtained from Pope Honorarius an audience for the
Templar Grand Master.

So Hugh de Payens set out for Rome in 1127, accompanied by a
small group of Templar knights, clerics and servingmen. The pope
received him warmly and summoned a great Council of the
church for the following year in the city of Troyes. There the Templars' elevation to a formal Order would be discussed and offered
for approval. Troyes was, of course, the family seat of Count
Hugh of Champagne, reflecting once again his benefactor's importance to the Templar cause.

But now the Grand Master's success with the pope meant he
had to move quickly. If he wanted his Templars to be taken seriously when he came before the Council, Hugh urgently needed to
recruit more men beyond the thirty knights already in his chival-
ric brotherhood. Equally important, he needed to put more
knights into the field in the Holy Land against the overwhelming
Muslim forces. This had to be done not just to achieve victories,
but to survive. And as a leader of knights, he was eminently quali-
fied to assess, inspire and enlist those men.

He also needed rich gifts from the kings and nobility of Europe
if he was to support and equip those knights in the Holy Land.
More than gold and silver, he needed lands and estates. Gold
could be spent only once, but land and estates could be farmed to
produce revenues year after year—and those streams of revenue
could be spent forever. Unfortunately, fundraising was an area he
was ill equipped to handle.

Hugh's lands and manor of Payns had come to him by right as
his father's son. He had no need to seek it, negotiate rights, define

Fig. 9   Saint Bernard

boundaries, or draw new contracts with peasants to farm the land and pay him appropriate rents. Moreover, begging for gifts of land was beneath the dignity of a member of French nobility. Not that such begging was not done, but disrepute often fell upon those who did it. He also lacked experience in determining the suitable amount to seek from a prospective donor, and how to tender the request appropriately to obtain a good response. Fortunately, he had people with him who were past masters at this enterprise: the brothers he had recruited in Lebanon.

These Lebanese brothers were descended from the master sea traders and businessmen of the Mediterranean world. The extent to which this Phoenician heritage was deeply imbued in their society was demonstrated as late as 1975 by Beirut being the financial capital of the Middle East. The ability of Lebanese entrepreneurs to charm a customer, negotiate an agreement, attend to appropriate details, and write a durable charter conveying property to its new owner was among the best in the East or in the West.

While in Northern France on this tour of recruitment, Hugh paid a critical visit to King Henry I of England—who was also the Duke of Normandy in France—at Henry's Norman estates. The *Anglo-Saxon Chronicle*, written by English scribes during those days, reported his meeting with the king this way.

> This same year (1128 AD), Hugh of the Temple came from Jerusalem to the king in Normandy, and the king received him with much honour, and gave him much treasure in gold and silver, and afterwards he sent him into England, and there he was well received by all good men, and all gave him treasure, and in Scotland also, and they sent in all a great sum in gold and silver by him to Jerusalem, and there went with him and after him so great a number [of knights] as never before since the days of Pope Urban.

Hugh continued onward to England as the king urged and was gifted with rich manors by different lords and ladies, including the Old Temple grounds in London. Those Old Temple lands were just south of High Holborn along Chancery Lane, and became the primary preceptory or headquarters for the Templars in England. The Templar knight they left behind to manage the estate became Prior—later called Master—of the Temple in England. With him were a number of administrative brothers who began to draw revenue from the other English estates and forward it to the Holy Land.

Meanwhile, the Grand Master and his remaining brothers continued northward into Scotland. There he received additional gifts of land that included the fair property of Balantrodoch south of Edinburgh. At that place he established his preceptory in Scotland, and commissioned a stone church that still stands today.

Hugh then returned to France to attend the Council of Troyes that had been promised to him by the pope. There he discovered Saint Bernard had prepared the stage well. Hugh was asked to describe for this council of church leaders the nature of the Knights Templar as well as their religious vows and practices. The strictness of their voluntary obligations pleased the assembled religious leaders, so they authorized Bernard to draw up a formal religious "Rule" to guide the Templars. This was a traditional step in officially forming a monastic order. Bernard was a "friend in court" for the Templars, so the Rule for them strongly resembled what they were already doing.

The Templar administrators who showed their value during the fundraising expedition held the title of chaplain, and now began to receive additional rewards alongside the knights. This was reflected in the Templar Rule.

> [Section] X.   Let a repast of flesh three times a week suffice you, excepting at Christmas, or Easter, or the feast of the Blessed Mary, or of All Saints…. On Sunday we think it clearly fitting and expedient that two messes of flesh should be served up to the knights and the chaplains. But let the rest, to wit, the esquires and retainers, remain contented with one, and be thankful therefor.

Having received the blessing of the council and the pope, Hugh set sail for the Holy Land at the head of many newly-recruited knights. Below decks his ships were laden with heavy loads of gold and silver. He left behind in France, England and Scotland small contingents of men to oversee the many scattered manors and lands that now belonged to his Order. Those brothers were charged with turning the properties into productive estates, and sending more boatloads of gold and silver to Jerusalem for support of this growing phenomenon that was the Knights Templar.

Ten years after the Council of Troyes, the pope recognized the escalating prominence of the Knights Templar by giving additional powers to them in his official letter *Omne datum optimum.* This remarkable document made the Templars exempt from the laws and rulers of every country, owing allegiance only to the pope. Their properties in different lands became part of an international domain that could not be touched.

The papal directive also granted a special reward for the clerical brothers in recognition of their critical services. Adding to their duties as chaplains, they were given all the rights and authorities of priests. They now put on their green robes and became a distinct third group among the Templars.

In further recognition of their services, the dean of the chaplains was granted extraordinary privileges. These included being seated immediately beside the Master at table, being served first, and other favored considerations.

This proved to be a critical milestone for the Templars and the secrecy in which they were starting to wrap themselves. Just as secrecy had been an essential part of Phoenician society, enabling them to survive life-threatening challenges for many centuries, it now began to play a greater role among the Templars.

This granting of priestly rights to the green-clad brothers finally allowed the Templars to eliminate outsiders from any role in their affairs. This included writing their private correspondence, recording their finances, or hearing their confessions in which all manner of things might be unburdened. They were at last able to draw the veil of secrecy firmly around their society.

The uniquely strong Templar tenets of secrecy, sworn oaths, unshakable brotherhood and other practices would deeply influence the conspiracy of knights that subsequently came into being.

King Richard the Lionheart

Richard Plantagenet who was called the Lionheart, allowed the crown of England to be placed upon his head in 1189. He was keenly aware that the throne had become his in tumultuous times. All of Europe reeled from the news that Jerusalem was now recaptured by the Muslim leader Saladin. Crusade fever was in the air. Richard threw himself immediately into preparing for this new Crusade and gathered his men around him. Soon thereafter he set sail at the head of a large army alongside his French ally, King Philip Augustus.

Richard's fiancée, Berengaria of Navarre, was hurrying to meet him when her ship became wrecked on the island of Cyprus. She was stranded there, only 100 miles from the Holy Land. Worse yet, the treasure aboard her ship was appropriated by King Isaac of Cyprus, who cast her and the other survivors into prison until he could decide what to do with them. Richard solved that problem for him by coming ashore in full rage with all his troops. He quickly conquered the entire island. Reunited with Berengaria once more, he married her on the spot.

With his personal needs satisfied he then sailed on to join the other Crusaders in the Holy Land. Richard arrived amid the thunder of warfare at the port of Acre, for the siege was already under way there against the Muslims who held the city. He chose to join the fray alongside the Knights Templar, in recognition of how far those knights had come. An almost mystical aura was beginning to surround the name and deeds of the Templar knights. One of Richard's men recorded the events as they happened.

At the period of the arrival of king Richard the Templars had again lost their Grand Master, and Brother Robert de Sablé or Sabloil, a valiant knight of the order, who had commanded a division of the English fleet on the voyage out, was placed at the head of the fraternity. The proudest of the nobility, and the most valiant of the chivalry of Europe, on their arrival in Palestine, manifested an eager desire to fight under the banner of the Temple. Many secular knights were permitted by the Grand Master to take their station by the side of the military friars, and even to wear the red cross on their breasts whilst fighting in the ranks.

The Templars performed prodigies of valour; "The name of their reputation, and the fame of their sanctity," says James of Vitry, bishop of Acre, "like a chamber of perfume sending forth a sweet odour, was diffused throughout the entire world, and all the congregation of the saints will recount their battles and glorious triumph over the enemies of Christ, knights indeed from all parts of the earth, dukes, and princes, after their example, casting off the shackles of the world, and renouncing the pomps and vanities of this life and all the lusts of the flesh for Christ's sake, hastened to join them, and to participate in their holy profession and religion."

On the morning of the twelfth of July, six weeks after the arrival of the British fleet, the kings of England and France, the christian chieftains, and the Turkish emirs with their green banners, assembled in the tent of the Grand Master of the Temple, to treat of the surrender of Acre, and on the following day the gates were thrown open to the exulting warriors of the cross. The Templars took possession of three localities within the city by the side of the sea, where they established their famous Temple, which became from thenceforth the chief house of the order. Richard Coeur de Lion…took up his abode with the Templars, whilst Philip resided in the citadel.[5]

In the months that followed, Richard rode alongside the Templars and scored many victories in the Holy Land. Yet the greatest prize of all eluded him. The city of Jerusalem did not fall. Even after two arduous campaigns it remained in Muslim hands. The most he could accomplish was to get Saladin to agree that Christians would have access to Jerusalem. He also gained confirmation of Christian control in the cities the Crusaders had captured.

Richard's last act in the Holy Land was to prepare for departure by dressing himself in the guise of a Templar knight. He did this to avoid his enemies, who would willingly hold him for ransom. Late in the year of 1192, Richard the Lionheart set sail for home.

Gilbert Erail, Philip de Plessis and the other Grand Masters of the Templars managed to maintain their Order's presence in the Holy Land during the years that followed. They held fast to their key cities and fortresses, sending out frequent forays along the normal pilgrim routes. Depending upon the strength or weakness of their adversaries over the years, there was an ebb and flow of control over the adjacent countryside.

Needless to say, the expenses they incurred for these exploits in the Holy Land were staggering. They faced a recurring need to provide horses, armor, retainers and ongoing provisions in this distant land. That created a growing need for revenue-producing estates. Fortunately, their white-clad knights and green-robed administrators had managed to ingeniously weave themselves into the social fabric so that their Order was an extremely popular recipient of gifts and bequests.

Fig. 10   Richard the Lionheart leaving the Holy Land

An astonishing enthusiasm was excited throughout Christendom in behalf of the Templars; princes and nobles, sovereigns and their subjects, vied with each other in heaping gifts and benefits upon them, and scarce a will of importance was made without an article in it in their favour. Many illustrious persons on their deathbeds took the vows, that they might be buried in the habit of the order; and sovereigns, quitting the government of their kingdoms, enrolled themselves amongst the holy fraternity, and bequeathed even their dominions to the Master and the brethren of the Temple.

Thus, Raymond Berenger, Count of Barcelona and Provence, at a very advanced age, abdicating his throne, and shaking off the ensigns of royal authority, retired to the house of the Templars at Barcelona, and pronounced his vows (A.D. 1130) before brother Hugh de Rigauld, the Prior. His infirmities not allowing him to proceed in person to the chief house of the order at Jerusalem, he sent vast sums of money thither, and immuring himself in a small cell in the Temple at Barcelona, he there remained in the constant exercise of the religious duties of his profession until the day of his death. At the same period, the Emperor Lothaire bestowed on the order a large portion of his patrimony of Supplinburg; and the year following (A.D. 1131) Alphonso the First, king of Navarre and Arragon, also styled Emperor of Spain, one of the greatest warriors of the age, by his will declared the Knights of the Temple his heirs and successors in the crowns of Navarre and Arragon, and a few hours before his death he caused this will to be ratified and signed by most of the barons of both kingdoms. The validity of this document, however, was disputed, and the claims of the Templars were successfully resisted by the nobles of Navarre; but in Arragon they obtained, by way of compromise, lands, and castles, and considerable dependencies, a portion of the customs and duties levied throughout the kingdom, and of the contributions raised from the Moors.[6]

Their resulting Templar empire came to extend over the full length of Europe, from Ireland to the Mediterranean. The Irish contribution increased when King Henry II became implicated in the murder of Saint Thomas Becket, the Archbishop of Canterbury. One of the ways this remorseful king made amends to the pope was to donate Clontarf Castle in Dublin to the Knights Templar. That prime property north of the Liffey River became the Templar preceptory in Ireland. As such, it took on the role of administering the other Irish properties that came to the Templars as well.

Surprisingly enough, Clontarf Castle not only still exists, it has been made into an elegant hotel in which one can sleep where the Templars slept—albeit in markedly better beds. The old Templar church still stands behind the castle, tucked away in a walled-off graveyard. Behind the church and castle rests part of the old jousting and exercise field, now converted into a public park. Standing among the few trees of the park, it is almost possible to hear the pounding of horses' hooves, the clash of metal on armor, and the chiming of the church bell, calling Templars to afternoon prayers.

And then there was Scotland.

Eight

Sir William de Beaujeu

Among the prized possessions held by the Grand Master of the Temple was the fine estate in Scotland originally given to Hugh de Payens. It spread across the countryside just a few miles from Rosslyn Chapel, and bore the unwieldy name of Balantrodoch. From there the Templars ruled other Scottish properties that included the Maryculter and Aboyne lands on the River Dee in Aberdeenshire, and significant estates at Nairnshire in the north country. There were also numerous smaller properties, some of which still bear the Temple name.

Far to the south in England, near the palaces of remorseful Henry II, the Master of the Temple in London expanded the Order's holdings from the relatively small property at High Holborn to a more commodious estate on the banks of the River Thames. Passage from the old site to the new was an easy five minute walk down Chancery Lane to Fleet Street—which formed the northern boundary of the fresh Templar estate. At the corner of Chancery and Fleet a pedestrian gateway opened to Inner Temple Lane, where a short walk down the path revealed the prize of the preceptory: the Temple Church. Patriarch Heraclius traveled from

Jerusalem to preside over the dedication ceremony for this re-markable place of worship.

This church—like several other Templar chapels—was built with a round tower in imitation of the Church of the Holy Sepulcher in Jerusalem. It reflected the circular enclosure around the tomb of Jesus and the place of his resurrection. That caused this part of Temple Church to be much in demand among Christian nobility and kings as a place to be buried. Adjacent to the round tower, just as in Jerusalem, was a long, rectangular chancel, with an altar dedicated to the Virgin Mary.

From this grand estate beside the Thames, the Master of the Temple administered manors and properties scattered over the length and breadth of England. These included Ewell in Kent, Daney in Cambridgeshire, Getinge in Gloucestershire, Cumbe in Somersetshire, Schepeley in Surrey, Samford in Oxfordshire, Garwy in Herefordshire, and Cressing in Essex.

Moving south across the English Channel to France, the holdings of the Grand Master were rich and plentiful, but in some degree of disarray. There were several different kingdoms in the land, and therefore several Templar preceptories. As the kings of Isle de France—meaning the area around Paris—expanded their holdings and acquired territories owned by other kings, they created a France similar to the one we know today. Responding to that change, the Templars accepted a suitable property in Paris around the year 1240 and raised a great fortress there. Armand de Périgord was Grand Master at that time, and made this impressive site in the heart of the city into his leading preceptory for France. Those remarkable grounds and buildings stood near today's Temple subway station in the 3rd arrondissement, just north of Notre Dame Cathedral. Its borders were the streets Rue du Temple, Rue de Bretagne, Rue Charlot, and Rue Béranger. From this grand edifice, the French Master of the Temple ruled a vast sea of estates that included Abbeville in the north; Nantes in the west; Marseille in the south; and Troyes in the west.

The Grand Master's preceptories in other countries likewise managed rich estates that contributed to the flow of funds coming to his headquarters in the Holy Land. Those holdings included Zaragoza in Spain, Tomar in Portugal, Templehof in Germany and

Fig. 11   Temple Church in London

Wielka Weis in Poland. Italy added Taranto and Brindisi, and Sicily contributed Syracuse and Messina. The parade of estates continued eastward to Greece, Cyprus and all across the Crusader states in the Holy Land.

As impressive as the extensive holdings of the Grand Master were—exceeding that of many kings—his Templar Order continued to be drained by the ongoing wars in the Holy Land. He found himself in need of still more sources of gold and silver.

So his men adopted and modified Near Eastern financial practices for the use of their Order—and created the equivalent of traveler's cheques in that early day and age. For most people in Europe this was a strange new concept. It was made possible by the many Templar preceptories scattered across the continent and all the way to Jerusalem. One of the great risks of travel in those days was thieves preying on people who carried enough gold and other valuables to finance long journeys through foreign lands. The Templars took that risk upon themselves, granting travelers the right to deposit their small fortunes at a preceptory near their home, and receive encrypted notes in return. These notes could then be presented at any Templar preceptory in any country along their journey—and the equivalent in silver coin or other money would be given to them. For this service the men of the Temple charged a reasonable fee that was gladly paid. The service became immensely popular, and this concept of bank checks became well established.

The enterprising Templars combined this with a multitude of other financial services, including the lending of money to kings and nobles to live their luxurious lifestyles and fight their wars. They also offered the well-guarded Templar strongholds as safe places to deposit valuable assets. These financial services became a massive business operation that was said to have eventually rivaled the Grand Master's main activity of fighting in the Holy Land.

Historians have frequently noted this unusual financial activity, but virtually never looked deeper to ponder how it came about. In truth, the knights among the Templars could not have done it. As pointed out by a scribe who recorded the minutes of the Council of Troyes in 1129, the two noble Counts who were present were illiterate. And a skill level far higher than simple literacy was required to keep the encrypted accounts and accurate financial records used for these services. Priests could read and write, but were prohibited by the church from engaging in moneylending. So who could possibly have done this?

The often-overlooked clerics among the Templars worked quietly behind closed doors to make it happen. These green-robed men had the proper roots to revive ancient financial practices and improve upon them. The Lebanese Christians among the Templar clerics belonged to a society whose international financial skills had developed over many generations. Their penchant for secrecy and numbers made the cryptic workings of these financial instruments a natural part of their work. They made it possible for the far-flung Templar empire to flourish.

So funds flowed and the Grand Master's campaigns in the Holy Land continued to be waged for decade after decade.

In the Holy Land, however, the day finally came when Muslim leaders were able to gather a tremendous force of soldiers and horsemen. With that accomplished, they set out to rid themselves of the infidels in their midst. One by one they began to extinguish the Christian strongholds. In the far north, Antioch fell in 1268. In Northern Lebanon, Tripoli was taken in 1289. Then their armies approached the critical lynchpin in the Crusader strongholds, the city of Acre, site of the Templar headquarters. The ensuing battle was epic in scale, with everything placed at risk. As the fighting became ever more desperate, the defenders' acts of valor bordered on the legendary.

Sir William de Beaujeu had guided the Templar knights through many battles during the eighteen years he served as their Grand Master. Now he led the defense of Acre for almost five weeks, holding out against the overwhelming number of attackers, until fate struck.

> A javelin came at the master of the Temple, just as he raised his left hand. He had no shield save his spear in his right hand. The javelin struck him under the armpit, and the shaft sank into his body a palm's length....

When he felt himself mortally wounded, he turned to go. Some of the defenders thought that he was retiring because he wanted to save himself. The standard-bearer saw him go, and fell in behind him, and then all of his household followed as well. After he had gone some way, twenty crusaders from the Vallo di Spoleto saw him withdrawing, and they called to him, "Oh for God's sake, Sir, don't leave, or the city will fall at once!" And he cried out to them in a loud voice, so that everyone could hear him: "My lords, I can do no more, for I am killed; see the wound here!"

And then we saw the javelin stuck in his body, and as he spoke he dropped the spear on the ground, and his head slumped to one side. He started to fall from his horse, but those of his household sprang down from their horses and supported him and took him off, and laid him on a shield that they found cast off there....

He did not speak again, but gave up his soul to God. He was buried before his tabernacle, which was the altar where they said mass. And God has his soul—but what great harm was caused by his death![7]

Yet even in the wake of William de Beaujeu's passing there was still a glimmer of hope.

The following morning very favorable terms were offered to the Templars by the victorious sultan, and they agreed to evacuate the Temple on condition that a galley should be placed at their disposal, and that they should be allowed to retire in safety with the christian fugitives under their protection, and to carry away as much of their effects as each person could load himself with. The Mussulman conqueror pledged himself to the fulfilment of these conditions, and sent a standard to the Templars, which was mounted on one of the towers of the Temple. A guard of three hundred Moslem soldiers, charged to see the articles of capitulation properly carried into effect, was afterwards admitted within the walls of the convent. Some christian women of Acre, who had refused to quit their fathers, brothers, and husbands, the brave defenders of the place, were amongst the fugitives, and the Moslem soldiers, attracted by their beauty, broke through all restraint, and violated the terms of the surrender. The enraged Templars closed and barricaded the gates of the Temple; they set upon the treacherous infidels, and put every one of them, "from the greatest to the smallest," to death.... The residue of the Templars retired into the large tower of the Temple, called "The Tower of the Master," which they defended with desperate energy. The bravest of the Mamlooks were driven back in repeated assaults, and the little fortress was everywhere surrounded with heaps of the slain. The sultan, at last, despairing of taking the place by assault, ordered it to be undermined. As the workmen advanced, they propped the foundations with beams of wood, and when the excavation was completed, these wooden supports were consumed by fire; the huge tower then fell with a tremendous crash, and buried the brave Templars in its ruins. The sultan set fire to the town in four places, and the last stronghold of the christian power in Palestine was speedily reduced to a smoking solitude.[8]

Just before the walls of Acre fell, some Templars led by Thibaud Gaudin saved a few of the people and what fortune of the Order remained in the city by spiriting them away to Sidon in Lebanon. Shortly after Acre's demise Sir Thibaud was elected the new Grand Master. Given the dire conditions confronting his men he felt compelled to order the remaining Templar strongholds at Sidon, Tortosa and Atlit be evacuated and left to the Saracens. The surviving Templars were ordered to fall back to the island of Cyprus and regroup there. This devastating loss of the Holy Land reverberated throughout the Knights Templar brotherhood and all of Europe.

Jacques de Molay

When Jacques de Molay was a young man in France he did not know that he would became Grand Master of the Knights Templar, nor that he would die tied to a stake and consumed in flames. All he knew was that his life was intertwined with Templars from the beginning. Jacques was born in rural France about eighty miles southeast of Troyes, the region that produced so many founding members of this knightly Order. Near his twenty-first birthday he finally became a Templar and gladly served in France for ten years before being sent to the Holy Land. There he became immersed in combat service and experienced the full rigors of a soldier's life. Having distinguished himself in the field, Jacques won assignment to England as Master of the Temple in London. Then came the news in 1291 that the Templars had lost their last foothold in the Holy Land and retreated to the island of Cyprus.

As soon as possible Jacques made his way to the East. Even so, he only arrived among the tattered Templar troops on Cyprus near the time Grand Master Theobald Gaudin passed away in 1292. De Molay was promptly chosen by his brethren to serve as the new Grand Master.

Fig. 12   Jacques de Molay, Grand Master

Surrounded by battered and scattered pieces of this once-proud Templar force, he forcefully set about retraining his fighting men. Jacques gave them a strong example to follow by strictly observing the articles of the Templar Rule. He also began to root out many of the shadowy practices that had crept into the Order during its long exposure to mysticism in the East.

He was aware of accusations about the Templars using unorthodox forms of secret worship, but those charges tended to be contradictory allegations about worshiping cats, idols, the devil, or heads. Of these, the only claim supported by any hint of evidence was the reverence shown to what was said to be the skull and crossed leg bones of the virgin martyr Saint Euphemia.

Yet he was not overly concerned about that because in those days there was great emphasis in the Catholic Church on collecting relics from saints. Altars were thought to be more holy if they contained a finger or fragment of bone recovered from a person who had been elevated to sainthood. Many Christian churches proudly displayed a severed hand, foot or head of a saint, instantly making their house of worship a place of local pilgrimage. In keeping with that tradition, the Templars were known to have collected many relics in their forays across the Holy Land, some of which eventually found their way into the hands of others.

> ...the Order, with its extensive eastern connections, built up a large collection of relics.... Relics were also used to strengthen links with potential patrons in the west and to maintain interest in the affairs of the Holy Land...in 1272 Thomas Bérard [the Templar Grand Master] sent to London pieces of the True Cross, together with relics of saints Philip, Helena, Stephen, Laurence, Euphemia, and Barbara.[9]

Given this widespread practice of venerating relics in churches, it is strange that the Templars would later be singled out for using relics in this manner, but that is what happened. In addition, Crusaders who lived in the Holy Land for any length of time were frequently said to adopt aspects of local dress, customs and practices. This may have included Kabbalah or other mystic Eastern practices that would have seemed quite strange to European observers. To the degree these Eastern rites were being practiced, Jacques sought to wean his men from them.

Yet the main mission de Molay set for himself was to obtain from the pope and the kings of Europe new support for a Crusade to retake the Holy Land. The long series of dispiriting failures in the later Crusades worked against him in this, but he was determined to push forward.

Among the obstacles in Jacques' way was Philip IV of France, one of the most powerful men in Europe. Philip was surnamed "the Fair" due to his handsome appearance—it was certainly not for any deference to justice on his part. And he had more important problems on his mind than the Crusades. Philip had acquired a crushing war debt and a lavish lifestyle, then made matters worse by beginning a new war with England. As his debt mushroomed out of control, the heavy-handed monarch began to aggressively tax his people and the Christian clergy in France.

Objecting to this taxation of the clergy, Pope Boniface VIII ordered that no such levy could be made without the consent of the pope. Philip responded by having the pope captured and so severely beaten that he died a month later.

The successor to Boniface was Benedict XI. This pope lived only eight months in office before dying under conditions often described as suspicious.

Philip then arranged to have a French archbishop chosen as pope. This was Clement V. The new pontiff apparently decided dying young was not appealing, and proceeded to give King Philip almost everything he wanted. As a sign of loyalty, Clement moved the seat of the Church from Rome to France, eventually settling at Avignon near Marseille.

Pope Clement was Jacques' direct superior. So when the pontiff proposed merging the Templars and Hospitallers into a single order, it put the Templar Grand Master in an extremely difficult position. To be fair, this idea was not original with Clement. Moreover, with no ongoing victories in the Holy Land, there was little justification to maintain two large military orders. Even so, this vexing proposal was another cross for Jacques to bear.

Fig. 13 The Templar preceptory in Paris

In a dark foreshadowing of events to come, King Philip fed his insatiable need for funds by arresting Italian bankers from Lombardy in 1291 and seizing their property. He applied the same harsh measures to Jews in France during 1306, pressing their assets into his treasury. That same year Philip admitted he had reduced the weight of silver coins in his realm, which ruined their value. Violent riots broke out in Paris and forced the king to take refuge in the fortress of the Templar preceptory. Unfortunately, the king's manipulation of the coinage of the realm created an immediate need for more gold and silver. And he had several days to sit in the richly appointed Templar buildings and think about where he might obtain it.

Yet Jacques was not concerned about those financial matters because he knew the real wealth of the Templars was not in the form of gold coins. It was their many estates acquired from noble benefactors over the years. These estates produced bountiful harvests, hand-made goods and revenues that were renewed each year. New gifts of silver, gold or lands had once been plentiful, but they had tapered off when the Holy Land was lost. Even so, the Order was well endowed.

The other leg upon which his financial powerhouse stood was the banking services his men offered to pilgrims, kings, and wealthy clients. It is true that the flow of pilgrims had largely dried up when protective knights were no longer stationed in the Holy Land. This left his men with banking and check-writing services limited largely to Europe. It also put more of the Templar resources into the up-and-down whims of kings and lords who took out loans or deposited tax revenues into the Templar vaults for safekeeping.

It was this last usage that probably created the impression of Templar preceptory vaults overflowing with money. Those making deposits, such as King Philip, could visit their piles of gold and silver in the vaults and make sure their bullion was still there. This no doubt gave the impression that all the other storage rooms were likewise piled high with riches. However that was rarely the case.

Jacques and his predecessors had never shown a desire to stockpile their riches in the West, even in the early days of the

Order. Their declared purpose was to raise every gold or silver coin they could find in Europe and send it East in the form of horses, armor, supplies or gold bullion to buy things they could not send. What they had was a flowing river of gold. It coursed from West to East, where the mouth of that gilded river sustained the body of the Order.

The headlands for his river of gold were the more than 870 estates collected by the Templars over their two centuries of existence. Each produced as much as possible in crops or other goods, then sold them in towns and markets to convert them into gold and silver coin. Each small bag of precious coins then needed to be picked up and brought to central collection points such as the Templar preceptories, where the modest, trickling streams became the river of gold that was needed.

The difficulty with this system was that people traveling with significant sums in those days were ready targets for highway robbery. Even single knights were at risk from bands of brigands. Two basic remedies were available at that time: strength and concealment. For the first, providing a body of knights to make the rounds was simple and effective. This was often done in the Templars' early days when the estates were few and the knights were plentiful. As the number of estates grew and the knights became desperately needed in the East, the use of concealment became more reasonable. This involved using unmarked couriers in plain clothes. As they made their rounds they would likewise stay at Templar-owned country houses or city residences that gave no outward Templar sign, nor betrayed any hint of the occasional bag of gold and silver coin passing through them. This invisible network required no traveling groups of knights to attend to it, and could be handled by the literate brethren who also managed the cryptic financial instruments offered to pilgrims. These green-robed men then quickly forwarded the funds to the East.

The other reason why Jacques did not leave large sums in Templar treasuries was that King Philip's attack on the Order in October of 1307 was not the first time their vaults had been raided. In 1285 the Templar treasury at Perpignan, France was broken into by Spanish King Peter III, who seized the funds left by his brother. In July of 1307, King Edward II of England broke into the

London Temple and took money, jewels and precious stones worth about £50,000. In short, the Grand Master was well aware that his treasuries were highly visible targets for powerful men. So he did not let funds collect in those stationary places but kept the river of gold flowing East.

Then in June of 1306 Jacques' prayers seemed to be answered. Pope Clement sent official letters to him and to Hospitaller Grand Master Foulques de Villaret announcing the pope's desire to receive their advice on proper steps for recovering the Holy Land! Both men were ordered to meet with the pope in France for this purpose.

For Jacques this was a moment of joy and elation. That he would agree to meet Clement was never in doubt. On the other hand de Villaret declined the pope's request. The leader of the Hospitallers offered the excuse that his campaign to capture the island of Rhodes was about to be launched. And in fact that siege did began the following year as promised.

De Molay kept his promise as well, going forth by boat in early 1307 to confer with Clement. He traveled first to Paris and deposited into Templar vaults some money he had brought to cover his expenses. The preceptories were apparently forwarding their funds to Cyprus so quickly that there was not enough in Paris to cover his living expenses. In any event Jacques was received with great ceremony by the king, then set off to Poitiers for meetings with the pope.

Meanwhile, Philip continued to weave his web around de Molay. The king's men were sent out to aggressively gather accusations against the Templars. They succeeded in finding a convicted criminal who charged the Templars with heresy and other terrible crimes in exchange for a full pardon from the king. Based on this and similar testimony, Philip issued his orders for the arrest of the Templars.

On that infamous Friday the 13th of October in 1307 Jacques was arrested along with those of his men in France who could be found. Many others escaped, but enough were seized to set Philip's plan in motion. The imprisoned knights and retainers at first denied the terrible charges against their Order. Then on the 19th of

October they were turned over to the Grand Inquisitor of the church.

This man brought to bear all the most feared tools of the Inquisition to work on the hapless Templars. The psychological damage was perhaps as terrible as the physical damage, for Jacques and the other Templars were in the service of the pope and had given him the best years of their lives. He now repaid those services with cruel and inhuman tortures to obtain confessions to imagined crimes.

It was no consolation to Jacques and his brothers, but this was not the first Inquisition. To combat the Cathars in Southern France—who believed there was corruption and improper use of sacraments in the Catholic Church—an Inquisition was mounted against them in 1184. That same fate awaited the Waldensians in Southern France and Northern Italy who preached a return to the simplicity of Jesus and the apostles. An Inquisition was launched against them in 1215. The Templars were next in 1307.

These Inquisitions and the ones that followed not only introduced the use of torture to attack suspected heretics, but raised this work to a high art form. The rack was used, the strappado, the waterboard, thumbscrews, fire and other imaginative means of torture were employed with skill. The objective was to obtain the desired confession without killing the victim, but the ferocity of the tortures naturally brought some number of deaths. Death more frequently came *after* the confession, as punishment.

One hundred and forty Templars were subjected to these extremities of torture in Paris. Among them was brother Bernarde de Vado who, when examined later by the commissary of police, explained part of his ordeal this way.

> They held me so long before a fierce fire that the flesh
> was burnt off my heels, two pieces of bone came
> away, which I present to you.[10]

Jacques survived. But thirty-six men died declaring their innocence and that of the Knights Templar. The other prisoners not only suffered physical damage, but also seem to have been shown forged letters from the Grand Master urging them to confess to guilt and end their ordeal. As a result, large numbers of the Templars gave confessions to the charges made against them and the Order. Later, away from the torture, many revoked their confessions; but the immediate effect was that they had given the king what he wanted.

With these forced confessions in hand, Philip went back to Pope Clement and demanded further action. Philip insisted the church support his actions by issuing a papal bull to all the other kings of Europe, ordering them to follow France's example and arrest all the Templars in their realms. Clement complied and sent that order a month later, requiring all Templars be held for trial. By the time those kings and rulers finally acted, however, only a handful of Templars could be found. The rest had disappeared.

But where did they go?

Chapter
Ten

Stephen of Safad

$\mathcal{S}$ir Himbert Blanke, the Grand Preceptor of Auvergne in France accompanied Jacques de Molay to Paris, but he managed to avoid Philip's arrests and made his way to England. Meanwhile in Scotland, Sir John de Hueflete was the Preceptor that land when the French arrests happened, and he disappeared along with many of his men. Of the roughly 4000 brothers in the Templar Order before the sudden arrests on Friday the 13th, only about 500 of those men appeared in the official records of arrests and trials in the East and West. What happened to the 3500 others?

The Templars in France may possibly have been given word of the planned attack on that day. If a tipster gave warning, however, the horrendous torture inflicted on captured brothers should have given some indication that was the case. The king of France was totally committed to his raid on the Templars, and would not have been lenient or quiet if there was even a hint of such betrayal. Yet no hue and cry went up among the French officers, and no traitor was brought forth. If no warning was given, that would make the puzzle of the knights' disappearance even more difficult to solve, but let us see where it leads.

Prior to King Philip's attack, brothers Himbert, John and all the other Templars were highly visible in public. They boldly wore their tunics of white with the blood-red Templar cross, appeared at public functions with their green-robed clerics, and were attended by a surrounding sea of brown-and-black-clad servingmen, all of whom bore the red Templar cross. There was no missing these men when they walked down a street, or charged across a battlefield in a mass of armor, uniforms and weapons.

Yet they also had a quiet and secretive side. It was in this mode that they conducted their clandestine meetings, lived their personal life, and handled their financial affairs. No one knew what they were doing, or when they were doing it. Their finances were wrapped in the tightest possible security by their clerical people so that not even King Philip—who displayed an intense interest in their financial affairs—knew when they were moving their funds nor how much they held in their treasuries.

Among the Templars, only the fewest number of people were privy to any particular secret. Even the Rules of their Order, the guidelines by which they lived, were not revealed to new members beyond what they needed to know. Only by living in the Order for many years did brothers gradually learn more of the Rule. Their meetings were not only off limits to outsiders, there were different levels of meetings. Servingmen could not participate in some of these, while other meetings were even more restricted. In their financial affairs, the "need to know" rule limited the number of brothers who were told which nondescript houses were in the invisible network through which their river of gold and silver flowed. Ideally, only the green-robed clerics who directly administered these finances would have known. When disaster struck on Friday the 13th, this financial network was part of the strong Templar fabric that answered the call of brothers in distress. Following the strict regimen of the Templar Order, they owed their highest duty to God and to their brothers in distress, whether on the battlefield or any other place. Those were the hallmarks of their Order, and took precedence over all other considerations.

When that disaster came, the few financial administrators who knew the location of these houses were obliged to tell the brothers around them. And as one brother discovered the location of such a safe house, he was required by his sworn obligations to tell others whom he knew positively to be brothers. The presence of severe danger would have caused the word of a secure place to cascade quickly to every branch and tendril of the Order.

Yet just as surely as they had an obligation to tell their fugitive brother of a safe place, the Templar injunction against telling such a secret to anyone who was not a brother was equally strict. This was ingrained in every facet of the Templar Order, from the legendary secrecy of their initiation rituals, to their chapter meetings where an armed guard stood at the door with a drawn sword. They believed that the lives of their brethren and the life of their Order hinged on keeping their secrets, even unto death. A leaked word about battle plans could kill a brother just as surely as leaving them alone on the battlefield. Neither of those was imaginable or acceptable in their tightly-knit society.

Only in a society such as this could the life-saving secret of an underground "railroad" of secure houses be passed so quickly to thousands of people, allowing them to safely step inside. Then just as suddenly they closed that door behind them. The men simply disappeared.

In the countries outside of France, there was no question that the Templars had clear warning of their impending fate. All the European monarchs refused to follow Philip's outrageous act of arresting members of the Templar Order. King Edward II of England even sent letters to many kings urging them not to give credence to those sordid charges.

However King Philip had gone too far to withdraw and realized the only way to justify his actions against the Templars was to force the other monarchs to attack them as well. So he compelled Pope Clement to issue the papal bull *Pastoralis praeemenentiae* demanding those arrests. In that letter Clement ordered the Templars be turned over to Church authorities for inquisition and trial. The pope's traditional hint of excommunication left those kings with little choice but to take action.

King Edward reluctantly had his English troops begin the arrest of Templars on the 8th of January 1308. Similar actions took place in Scotland and Ireland. But by then almost three months had passed since the arrest of Templars in France, so these brothers had ample warning of what would befall them. In large groups or one-by-one, most of the British Templars disappeared into the underground railroad that carried brothers to safety. Having reached those clandestine places, these fugitives were temporarily protected. But then where did they go?

The pope provided a path by ordering all Templars to join the Hospitallers. Unfortunately his word did not carry much weight with the Templars by this time. Perhaps it had something to do with the tortures applied by the pope's inquisitors. In any event, relatively few in Europe seem to have chosen that option.

In fairness to the pope, his proposed path suffered other difficulties as well. The Hospitallers had been nose-to-nose rivals of the Templars for almost two hundred years. Across the battlefields of the Holy Land and the courts of Europe the two orders had struggled on an almost daily basis trying to out-do the other. The thought of casting aside Templar white and donning Hospitaller black would have been almost unimaginable even in the best of times, and these were not the best of times.

The pope's order that all Templar lands likewise be given to the Hospitallers fared no better. Despite aggressive pursuit of these lands by the Hospitallers and papal authorities, there was rampant confusion. King Edward and other secular authorities laid claim to a number of these properties, and many other claims were disputed all across Europe. The number of Templars coming to the Hospitaller standard was so small that there appeared to be minimal support or records on hand for the men in black as they tried to take ownership of these prizes.

On Cyprus the Templar afflictions played out much differently. Stephen of Safad was one of the Templars who remained on duty at this makeshift headquarters of their Order. He was well aware of the ongoing skirmishes between his brothers and the Hospitallers, and the great aggravation this brought to the king of Cyprus. And it only became worse when the pope's order to arrest the Templars arrived in May of 1308. By that time Stephen was among only eighty-three Templar knights and thirty-four servingmen left on the island. He was the lone clerical brother, highly noticeable in his green robe with the red cross.

Hundreds of his brothers had already departed this once-bustling center amid great secrecy. He knew because he was one of the clerical brothers who made it possible. The financial network he administered had many safe locations that he recently had been giving to any brother who asked. What happened to them beyond that point was up to other brothers and to God. He arranged passage for them on ships, saw them off, and they disappeared.

His clerical brothers were among the first who left in this manner. They had to convert the financial safe houses for use by all the brothers who followed. Yet one of their number had to remain behind to wear the green robe that was a beacon for brothers seeking asylum. Stephen chose to do that duty because his life was here. He was born on the border between Lebanon and Israel, and continued the long tradition of Lebanese Christians who joined the Templars. Like his forebears, his skill was not in military matters but in the business affairs for which his people were famous. Now he would be the last of his line to serve as a clerical brother. And he knew that when all the Templars around him had their needs met, he would have to make his own decision.

He stood trial alongside his Templar brothers on Cyprus. But after due examination by the inquisitors, no evidence of guilt was found. So no punishments were ordered. He waited in limbo with his brothers, hoping some good news might come. But then in 131 came the papal bull *Vox in excelso* that disbanded the Templar Order. With it came extreme pressure from the Vatican for him and for his brothers on Cyprus to convert to the Hospitallers. Helping to push them in this direction was the success of the long Hospitaller siege at Rhodes. That Greek island had fallen to the black knights in August of 1309, allowing them to build encampments in a land where they faced no competition from other lords. For any Templars desiring to continue their military life, this offer was a compelling one, and Stephen did not begrudge any of his brothers on Cyprus who chose to go this way. After submitting the proper records for those brothers, he bundled the rest of the records so that they looked like trade goods. Then he chartered a boat, loaded his consignment of goods, and simply disappeared.

In Europe there were more appealing choices for the battered Knights Templar, with one of them being offered by King Dinis of Portugal. He knew the kings before him had a long and mutually beneficial relationship with the Templars, and he wanted to keep it working to his advantage.

The early *Reconquista* had recovered about half of Portugal from the Muslims by 1128, the year in which Hugh de Payens had come to Europe. The first Grand Master of the Templars had been seeking lands to support his new order and Queen Theresa of Portugal gave him the town of Fonte Arcada, asking in return that the Templars attempt to conquer more territory from the Muslim forces. Hugh's knights dutifully complied and in 1159 were rewarded with the lands of Ceras and Tomar in central Portugal, roughly halfway between the cities of Lisbon and Porto. There they built the Castle of Tomar with its famous round church, the *Convento de Cristo*. It was a match made in heaven.

King Dinis was not about to give that up to please the king of France or the pope in Rome. So he ignored the pope's letter demanding the arrest of the Templars. That resistance prompted Pope Clement to issue another papal bull called *Regnas in coelis* the following year, ordering Dinis to investigate the Templars in his lands. Dinis did so, and then in 1310 joined with the neighboring king of Castile to declare the Templars innocent in the Iberian peninsula.

Clement raised the ante by sending Dinis and the king of Castile copies of his papal bull in 1312 suppressing the Templar Order, followed a few months later by the order to turn over all Templar property to the Hospitallers. But Dinis was determined not to let anyone outside of Portugal take control of these prized lands. So he created a new military brotherhood, the Order of Christ, into which he accepted all of the Portuguese Templars. He then invested this new order with all the Templar lands in Portugal. In other words, he allowed the Knights Templar to continue operating in Portugal just as before. The only change was in the name carved over their door.

Fig. 14 The Templar castle at Tomar in Portugal

King Dinis expressed no reservations about allowing Templars from other parts of Europe to join this new order, but very few came. More than eleven years had elapsed since King Philip's attack, so most of the Templars in other lands had already moved on and found an acceptable course for their life.

Another unusual but intriguing path was taken by Bernard of Fuentes and some of the other outlawed Templars. He was not known to be a pirate himself, but he became a brother to pirates and corsairs.

Ever since the time of Richard the Lionheart, when the Templar Grand Master moved his headquarters to the seaport city of Acre, the Templars had possessed a significant navy. Their ships were frequently seen in European ports, as well as ports in the Middle East and North Africa. When the order went out from King Philip to arrest Jacques de Molay and his knights in France, and seize their possessions, the Templar ships simply put out to sea and were never seen again.

At that point each Templar captain was master of his ship and crew. He could sail to any port where arrest warrants had not yet gone out. Unfortunately that list became shorter when the pope extended the arrest order to all Christian countries. With his men and himself running risk of imprisonment each time he put into port, the captain could have sold his ship at the next port and retired to a comfortable house on the shore. No doubt some did. On the other hand, if he continued to sail with a writ out against him, he was an outlaw with limited options—such as smuggling contraband or other forms of outright piracy.

The havens for such piracy were largely in non-Christian ports, where the pope's orders of arrest had no standing. Perhaps by coincidence the rate of piracy increased in the ports of Tunis, Tripoli and Algiers along the Muslim-occupied shores of North Africa. Known as the Barbary Coast, this stretch of land eventually gave rise to the Barbary pirates.

Bernard of Fuentes was a Spanish Templar who disappeared when the attacks on his Order began, then reappeared in a different guise.

Channels of communication with the north African powers were, in fact, well established, and it would not have been all that surprising to the Aragonese [in Spain], when, in September 1313, Bernard of Fuentes, former Preceptor of Corbins, turned up at the court of James II in Barcelona as the ambassador of the Muslim ruler of Tunis.[11]

Alongside other signs of piracy, one of the most popular flags under which those pirates sailed bore a striking resemblance to the Templar flag, as well as to one of the knights' more esoteric practices. The "Jolly Roger" banner became famous as a black flag bearing a white skull and two crossbones. The flag carried into battle by Templar knights was called the *Beauceant*, and consisted of two panels, one black and one white. As we have seen, the Templars were also known for collecting relics of Christian saints. One of their most treasured relics was said to be the skull of St. Euphemia, which was displayed in ceremonies with her two crossed leg bones. Some have argued that the bones were not those of St. Euphemia, but it is now widely accepted that the Templars revered the skull and crossed bones of some deceased donor during their private ceremonies.

But not all the paths that were open to fugitive Templars were so far away or exotic. Many men in England, Scotland and Ireland were going forward in ways closer to home.

Sir John de Hueflete

John de Hueflete was the Templar Preceptor of Scotland when brothers fleeing France began to arrive at his Balantrodoch estate. Hearing that his Grand Master was confined to a French prison and Pope Clement was not angrily rising to the defense of the Templar Order, Sir John feared the end was near. His first concern was to find suitable hiding places for his French guests, for they were fugitives from the law and from their pope.

He called on his green-robed clerics and charged them to care for these brothers by putting them in safehouses. When the French Templars were securely situated, he asked his diligent administrators to redouble their efforts and expand the quickly-growing clandestine system to accommodate all the other Templars under his command. Word soon arrived that other Templar preceptories in England and Ireland were doing the same. When he could wait no longer Sir John left Walter de Clifton and another knight to attend to Templar interests in Scotland, gathered his other men around him, and disappeared.

In France some Templars were already dying, and there was no way to know when the same might start in Britain. Even so, Sir John looked after his French brothers and Sir Walter stayed behind so that his brothers could live. Each of them took these risks willingly. Honor and survival meant something different to Templars than it did to most people.

They had faced death on the battlefield, on open roads in the Holy Land, and in quiet towns that suddenly exploded into fighting. In all those situations, the one thing they could cling to with certainty was the unbreakable bonds they shared with their brothers. Their brothers would always be there for them. Death would come sooner or later. But when it came, they wanted it to be with honor, knowing they had stood by their brethren, just as their brothers had stood by them.

Even the unusual and widely-recognized symbol of the Knights Templar—two knights upon a single horse, reflected their ultimate commitment to brotherhood. It was often said that this symbol showed them as being poor soldiers of Christ, unable to afford a second horse. That made no sense, of course. Even in their earliest and poorest days, the Rule of the Templars allotted to each knight several horses.

> To each one of the knights let there be allotted three horses. The noted poverty of the House of God, and of the Temple of Solomon, does not at present permit an increase of the number, unless it be with the license of the Master....
>
> Section XXX of the Templar Rule

Another clue that this unique symbol proudly displayed by the Templars did not denote poverty was that the Templars were one of the richest societies that ever existed. Their wealth and properties extended from the Middle East to Western Europe. Individual knights could not own personal property of any value, such as gold chains or silver dishes. But as members of their Order they had castles, armor, horses and the like in great profusion, and wanted for nothing. Poverty was not what made them exceptional.

The only time one could have seen two Templar knights on a single horse would be upon their return from the battlefield. If one knight's horse died in battle, and the man faced imminent death

Fig. 15   The Templar seal

on foot surrounded by the enemy, no other knight was allowed to leave the field of battle. The nearest knight was obliged by stubborn honor to fly to the aid of his brother, no matter the cost. I believe it is that loyal knight, having rescued his brother, whom we see returning after battle with his fellow knight seated behind. That was the symbol of the Templars. To them, it embodied their pride, honor, and lifelong bond of brotherhood.

As Sir John demonstrated, the Templar estates became critically important at that moment. Some of the larger estates were well-known to the people of that day. Yet it was also true that many Templar holdings were much smaller and less well-known. These latter properties could change hands frequently, making ownership unclear even to their neighbors. Malcolm Barber, a well-respected chronicler of the Templars, noted that:

> ...the Order was not simply a passive recipient of donations, but an active agent in the land market, buying, selling and exchanging property on a considerable scale.[12]

This practice made it difficult for anyone other than a Templar scribe to know which properties belonged to their Order. Desired properties and buildings could be purchased, and then passed through the hands of several people who may or may not have actually existed. After that, the property was available for use in the Templars' clandestine financial system. Such properties were not on the Templars' books, and any tracks that might have been left behind were soon lost in the flurry of transactions. These houses and lands were safe indeed.

During the Templars' hour of need the treasuries of the northern preceptories seemed to be as bare as those of the French. But their river of gold still flowed. Sir Walter and the senior officers in other preceptories insured that collections from every estate, great and small, went on as before. But now with the Grand Master in a French prison and the survival of their Order in doubt, there was no reason to send the funds forward. Like an army foraging for supplies before a battle, they also performed the systematic stripping of Templar estates to remove everything of value. This was the final, great harvest.

All those funds were needed immediately to lodge, conceal and feed the continuing flow of brothers going into hiding. Rooms needed to be added onto covert houses. Supplies needed to be laid in. Additional safe houses or inns near cities needed to be purchased in preparation for immediate use if the dreaded order to arrest all Templars came down in Britain.

In fact, one of the most famous of all English inns, known as the Tabard, was built that same year in Southwark, just across the River Thames from London. It stood near the south end of London Bridge. This was the inn Geoffrey Chaucer described in the opening lines of *The Canterbury Tales*, when he told of people gathering there for their pilgrimage to Canterbury.

> *Befelle that in that season, on a day,*
> *In Southwerk, at the Tabard as I lay*
> *Redy to wenden on my pilgrimage*
> *To Canterbury, with devoute couràge....*[13]

The Tabard was not a Templar inn, since it was built for religious brothers at the Abbey of Hyde. Yet it shows religious brothers owned inns during those days without being out of the ordinary. Even better, it was customary at that time for each inn to actually be a collection of buildings completely encircling a private yard. Riders could dismount there and wagons be quietly unloaded. This gave privacy to their "guests," who never need be seen by the people in neighboring establishments.

Sir Walter and the others had to do all these things in great haste because they were running out of time.

Sir Walter on Trial

In service to his hidden brothers Sir Walter remained at his post and kept the river of gold flowing as long as possible. He also kept alive his Order's claim to its property and place in Scottish society. If somehow the angel of death were to pass over them, and the Templar Order miraculously survived, he would be there at the door to welcome back the many brothers who had laid down their mantles and swords to go into hiding.

Unfortunately, there was no passover that year. The arrests in Britain finally began. And just as Philip had done before him, King Edward's labors in England produced only a small portion of all the Templars in the land—two hundred and twenty-nine by actual count.

In Scotland the count was even smaller. A total of two were arrested: Sir Walter and his fellow knight Sir William de Middleton. The two men were hosted in bleak cells by the pope's inquisitors. Then the trial finally began on the 17th of November 1309 at Holyrood Abbey in Edinburgh. The inquisitors' insistent questioning allowed church scribes to record Sir Walter's description of heretofore secret Templar practices, including the sacrosanct ritual of initiation.

He states that they then led him to the chamber of the Master, where they held their chapter [meeting], and that there, on his bended knees, and with his hands clasped, he again prayed for the habit and the fellowship of the Temple; that the Master and the brethren then required him to answer questions to the following effect: Whether he had a dispute with any man, or owed any debts? Whether he was betrothed to any woman? And whether he had any secret infirmity of body? Or knew of anything to prevent him from remaining within the bosom of the fraternity? And having answered all those questions satisfactorily, the Master then asked of the surrounding brethren, "Do ye give your consent to the reception of brother Walter?" who unanimously answered that they did; and the Master and the brethren then standing up, received him the said Walter in this manner. On his bended knees, and with his hands joined, he solemnly promised that he would be the perpetual servant of the Master, and of the order, and of the brethren, for the purpose of defending the Holy Land. Having done this, the Master took out of the hands of a brother chaplain of the order the book of the holy gospels, upon which was depicted a cross, and laying his hands upon the book and upon the cross, he swore to God....

Being asked where he had passed his time since his reception, he replied that he had dwelt three years at the preceptory of Blancradok [Balantrodoch] in Scotland; three years at Temple Newsom in England; one year at the Temple at London, and three years at Aslakeby. Being asked concerning the other brothers in Scotland, he stated that John de Hueflete was Preceptor of Blancradok, the chief house of the order in that country, and that he and the other brethren, having heard of the arrest of the Templars, threw off their habits and fled, and that he had not since heard aught concerning them.

Brother William de Middleton, being examined, gave the same account of his reception....

After the examination of the above two Templars, forty-one witnesses, chiefly abbots, priors, monks, priests, and serving men, and retainers of the order in Scotland, were examined upon various interrogatories, but nothing of a criminatory nature was elicited. The monks observed that the receptions of other orders were public, and were celebrated as great religious solemnities, and the friends, parents, and neighbours of the party about to take the vows were invited to attend; that the Templars, on the other hand, shrouded their proceedings in mystery and secrecy, and therefore they *suspected* the worst.... The serving men and the tillers of the lands of the order stated that the chapters were held sometimes by night and sometimes by day, with extraordinary secrecy.[14]

When the trial in Scotland ended with no guilt being found, Sir Walter returned to the Templar manor house in Balantrodoch, put his affairs in order, mounted his horse and disappeared. Not long thereafter he was among his hidden brothers again.

William de la More was the Master who initiated Sir Walter as a Templar ten years earlier. Now as Master of the Temple in London he was the senior knight in all of England. Even so he gave himself no exemption from duty and, like Sir Walter, stayed at his post to be arrested and lead the local defense of his Order.

After languishing many months in prison, his trial and that of the other knights in London began on the 20th of October 1309. He was among the forty-three Templars—plus seven witnesses from outside the order—who were called to testify. He resolutely denied all the charges, as did the others. Having failed to find damning evidence, the inquisitors petitioned King Edward to let the Inquisition have greater freedom to extract "the truth" from Sir William and the other Templars. The king reluctantly authorized this to be done, sending such orders on the 16th of December to his sheriffs holding Templars at London, Lincoln and York. Even so, the methods used were not too excessive and the trials lingered for another year.

In frustration Pope Clement wrote to King Edward and chastised him for not allowing the Inquisition to use the rack and similar tortures in performance of their duties. With that, Edward capitulated completely. His order on in August of 1310 directed the constable of the Tower and all the sheriffs to turn their Templars over to the inquisitors, and permit those men to do to the bodies of the Templars whatever they felt was necessary. To their credit, the English jailers seem to have been reluctant to follow such grisly instructions, for the king had to send his orders twice more, each time more sharply than the last, requiring they turn the Templars over for torture.

Despite the agonies endured by Sir William and his brethren, the next set of trials still produced no confessions. So the level of punishment and privation was raised higher. Almost a year later, in June and July of 1311, breakthroughs were achieved. Two servingmen of the order as well as a chaplain finally buckled under the Inquisition and gave their confessions.

After four years of fruitless efforts in England, the church leaders conducting the trials accepted those three confessions as all they were going to get. Accordingly, they arranged a compromise whereby any Templar could simply attest that the Master in their Order might have given absolution for sins, which he had no right to do, and ask forgiveness for this and any other heresy. Since this vague statement amounted to virtually no confession at all, most of the brothers immediately agreed to it, received absolution from the church, and were set free. They were then able to simply disappear as their brothers had done.

Only William de la More, Master of the Temple in England, and a few of his men refused even that minor statement. He finally died in solitary confinement in the Tower of London.

In France, the ordeal of the Templars took a nasty turn. Peter of Bologna and many other Templars had given confessions under duress in order to end the torment and gain their freedom. This gave the French king enough justification to destroy their Order and seize its property, so he let the shattered and disgraced men receive absolution from the church for their "crimes" and released them from prison. But by 1310, Peter and his brothers had regained their health and heard how their brethren in England and other lands were steadfastly refusing to accept the charges against them. As a result, he now renounced those statements and proclaimed his innocence. Many other Templars in France joined him. When they did that, their well-concealed brothers were no longer able to shield them. The whole idea of being hidden meant one did not make public statements or become publicly visible. Yet these men deeply regretted having given in to the torture and felt compelled to go public.

Their new declarations undercut everything Philip was trying to accomplish. Furious, he ordered the arrest of Peter and the other rebellious Templars. He then arranged for the Archbishop of Sens to pass death sentences on them, which the prelate did in this manner.

> "You have avowed that the brethren who are received into the order of the Temple are compelled to renounce Christ and spit upon the cross, and that you yourselves have participated in that crime: you have thus acknowledged that you have fallen into the sin of *heresy*. By your confession and repentance you had merited absolution, and had once more become reconciled to the church. As you have revoked your confession, the church no longer regards you as reconciled, but having fallen back to your first errors. You are, therefore, *relapsed heretics* and as such, we condemn you to the fire." [15]

The next day, on the 12th of May 1310, Peter and fifty-three other Templars were taken to the Porte St. Antoine des Champs at Paris, and were burned to death.

Over the months that followed, dozens of other Templars were rounded up and forced to reaffirm their confession under penalty of life in prison or death. Many, perhaps shamed by their earlier weakness, accepted the penalty. Altogether, a total of a hundred and thirteen Templars were reported as burned at the stake in

Paris, with others being burned in Lorraine, Normandy, Carcassonne and Senlis.

Dante's Inferno

Dante Alighieri was moved by the flaming deaths and suffering of the Templars to write his famous *Inferno*, which explored the depths of hell. Born in Florence during 1265, he received only a modest education but was a prodigious reader of classical works and poetry. By age eighteen he was already sitting with other young writers and gave rise to a new literary style that became highly popular in Italy. This enabled him to make a good living with his pen, but it was his dabbling in politics that soon came to dominate his life.

Florence was only 140 miles from the Vatican and the strong influence of the popes chafed some of the Florentines. Two rival factions sprang up, and Dante sided with those who wanted to keep his city independent of the pope. When the Vatican began planning a military intervention, the city sent Dante and other influential citizens to meet with the pope and head off any attack. Dante was somewhat shocked when the pope put him under virtual house arrest in Vatican City after dismissing his fellow protesters.

That feared invasion took place in 1301 when papal representative Charles of Valois, aided by local supporters, destroyed much of Florence and killed many of Dante's compatriots. Among the survivors was young Salvestro de' Medici, whose family had not yet made its mark in the city—but when they did, the mark would be indelible. For now, the pope's loyal supporters were the government, and they banned Dante from the city he knew and loved. It was a bitter pill to swallow, and Dante had to rely on the hospitality of friends in other Northern Italian cities for the rest of his life.

When Templars were attacked by the pope six years later, Dante identified with the agony of the knights and rallied to their cause. After several failed attempts against the Templars in Italy, Pope Clement ordered his bishops to try once more to win convictions for heresy. He directly urged the use of torture "to be more certain to elicit the truth".[16]

So thirteen Templars were arrested in Tuscany and five of them came to trial at St. Gilles church in Florence. The infliction of pain seemed to be effective, since all five confessed to various improprieties, as did a sixth Templar on trial in Lucca. This turned out to be a form of well-managed theater, since the other seven Templars had insisted on their innocence—and therefore were not brought to trial to make those public statements. A separate note recorded that their "responses or denials" had been given "although we have exposed them to questions and tortures".[17]

The suffering and fiery death of many Templars filled Dante with a passionate mission. He sat down to write, and the *Inferno* came pouring out. This epic poem's popularity came about largely due to the symbolic language he used so masterfully. That indirect communication was almost mandatory, since he was writing about people still living or recently dead. Pope Clement V died while Dante was writing, and he sent the man directly to hell. Clearly he could not do that to him by name, since Clement was followed in that powerful office by other popes capable of sending a poet or two to hell in a very real way. So he used symbolic language to veil his work from the authorities.

As Dante passed through hell he identified a specific place reserved for Pope Clement whom he described as "pastor sanza legge" or the lawless shepherd. And upon noting that popes after Clement were still serving the French kings, he identified them as

Fig. 16   Dante's Inferno

"puttaneggiar coi regi" or prostitutes of the king. In his shoes, given what had just happened to the Templars, we would probably write that in coded form also. Dan Brown makes generous use of Dante's cryptic messages during the adventures that take place in his own *Inferno* book.

Even though Pope Clement had found no real evidence against the Templars other than the bits and pieces we have seen, he still abolished the Templar Order. He took that momentous step on the 22nd of March 1312, in his papal bull *Vox in excelso*. He closed the door on this Order and cast out its fugitive brothers to make their own way in the world as best they could.

Despite that closure, Jacques de Molay and a handful of his brothers remained in prison. From time to time he was trotted out to publicly confess again, in a futile effort by King Philip and Pope Clement to justify their actions. At one such display on the 18th of March 1314, everything went horribly wrong.

> A public scaffold was erected before the cathedral church of Notre Dame, at Paris, and the citizens were summoned to hear the Order of the Temple convicted by the mouths of its chief officers, of the sins and iniquities charged against it. The four knights, loaded with chains and surrounded by guards, were then brought upon the scaffold by the provost, and the bishop of Alba read their confessions aloud in the presence of the assembled populace. The papal legate then, turning towards the Grand Master and his companions, called upon them to renew, in the hearing of the people, the avowals which they had previously made of the guilt of their order. Hugh de Peralt, the Visitor-General, and the Preceptor of the Temple of Aquitaine, signified their assent to whatever was demanded of them, but the Grand Master raising his arms bound with chains towards heaven, and advancing to the edge of the scaffold, declared in a loud voice, that to say that which was untrue was a crime, both in the

sight of God and man. "I do," said he, "confess my guilt, which consists in having, to my shame and dishonour, suffered myself, through the pain of torture and the fear of death, to give utterance to falsehoods, imputing scandalous sins and iniquities to an illustrious order, which hath nobly served the cause of Christianity. I disdain to seek a wretched and disgraceful existence by engrafting another lie upon the original falsehood." He was here interrupted by the provost and his officers, and Guy, the Grand Preceptor, having commenced with strong asseverations of his innocence, they were both hurried back to prison.

King Philip was no sooner informed of the result of this strange proceeding, than, upon the first impulse of his indignation, without consulting either pope, or bishop, or ecclesiastical council, he commanded the instant execution of both these gallant noblemen. The same day at dusk they were led out of their dungeons, and were burned to death in a slow and lingering manner upon small fires of charcoal which were kindled on the little island in the Seine, between the king's garden and the convent of St. Augustine, close to the spot where now stands the equestrian statue of Henry IV.[18]

In this manner the official existence of the Knights Templar came to an end. Several hundred of the brethren had died, some agonizingly and in flames.

Yet Walter de Clifton and many of his brothers still lived in places of hiding. They had been shaped by the Templar Order to live in a world based on brotherhood, obligations, meeting in secret, and being part of something greater than themselves. Now they had to adapt and join their old life to a new one. And they began to shape a rebellion against the kings and Vatican that had done these unspeakable things to them.

Their lives also changed in another way. As Templars they had been single men, bound by oaths of chastity and duty to the

Fig.17   Jacques de Molay being burned at the stake

church. Now they sought a more normal life. They took wives and began to raise families of their own. By so doing it soon became evident they had more to protect than they did before.

Yet Sir Walter and his brothers were not the first to make this change from single knight to head of a household, and founder of a family line. One of those who had done it before was William St. Clair, who began the famous family that built Rosslyn Chapel. His family's experiences reveal the challenging world into which the battered but determined Templars now had to make their way.

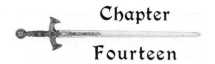
Sir William St. Clair

As a young man William St. Clair came to England from Normandy alongside William the Conqueror in 1066. After those heady victories he was still a landless and unattached knight errant, so he accepted an offer from the king of Scotland to seek his fortune in that northern land. At Edinburgh he entered the service of the royal family and soon made his mark. Known as "The Seemly St. Clair" for his strikingly handsome appearance, William became Queen Margaret's cup-bearer or steward. His ability to win her favor persuaded King Malcolm to confer upon him the Barony of Roslin.

Sir William's beautiful new estate was located on the southern approach to Edinburgh, just nine miles from the heart of the city. The young knight then had the good sense to marry Dorothy, daughter of the earl of Dunbar, which tied him even closer into the nobility of Scottish society. Dorothy soon bore him a son named Henry. His son had just reached his sixteenth birthday when Sir William set out once more to do battle for his king and tragedy struck. William died in a clash of arms on a field not far from home.

So Henry became the 2nd Baron of Roslin at this tender age. But he was an experienced knight nine years later when the First Crusade was mounted in 1096. He traveled to the Holy Land with that large body of troops and fought in the same campaigns as a knight who was only a year older than himself, Hugh de Payens — who would go on to be the first Templar Grand Master. After three long years of battle Henry finally stood inside the walled city of Jerusalem with the other victorious knights. But then, just like most of the others, he decided his duty was done and no longer bound him to stay in the Holy Land. He returned home to the green hills of Roslin, and to the service of the Scottish king.

Sir Henry was fifty-seven by the time Hugh de Payens came to Scotland in 1128 on his mission to collect men and estates to support the newly-established Knights Templar. The king of Scotland, David the First, generously donated the lands of Balantrodoch only four miles east of Roslin.

Henry was not in a position to make such extravagant gifts himself. But when he heard Sir Hugh wanted the landed gentry to give financial support towards Balantrodoch's expenses, or provide aid to that preceptory in time of need, it was impossible for him as a former comrade-in-arms to refuse.

To discover how difficult it might be to travel from the manor house at Roslin to the one at Balantrodoch, I walked that distance during an exploratory trip to Roslin. It was possible to hike comfortably between the two residences in a couple of hours — a distance that could easily have been covered on horse-back in about thirty minutes. The St. Clairs and the newly-created Knights Templar could have come to each other's dinner table in a half hour's time, and would be able to do so for the next 184 years.

Sir Henry was succeeded as Baron of Roslin by his son, also named Henry, who made an important contribution to his family by building the first St. Clair castle. When he hired masons to begin laying stones, he had no way to know this would one day be the site of Rosslyn Chapel. He just wanted a respectable manor house of durable stone for his family. One of the most remarkable features of this first castle was its small chapel downstairs. It was simply adorned with perfectly-cut ashlar stones and a rounded ceiling. We know this because it is still there. Inside Rosslyn

Chapel today are old steps leading down to this modest but ancient place of prayer, now known as the Lower Chapel. This first
stone manor was completed in 1210 and housed his family in a
proper fashion befitting a Scottish baron.

Henry followed the traditional practice among noble families
of ensuring the whole of his lands would pass to his eldest son.
The alternative would be to splinter the estate among all his children, but that practice inevitably led—in a few generations—to
members of noble families being reduced to commoners in all but
name.

This gave rise to the common practice whereby noble families
pushed non-inheriting sons into religious orders such as the Benedictines or Franciscans. The vows of chastity accompanying this
monkhood or priesthood also meant those sons lived out their
lives without having children—an additional boon in terms of
avoiding future claimants. This in turn led to one of the strongest
attractions of the Knights Templar among the younger nobility.
The Templars were a religious order that had the same difficult
vows of chastity and obedience. But for the young man being
prodded into religious service by his family, it was a colorful and
exciting military alternative to drab monkhood in some quiet abbey.

Lineage records clearly show the St. Clair family had many
younger sons who did not inherit the family's titles and estates.
Unfortunately, all that is known about most of these younger sons
is their name, rather than the course they took in life. So there is
no way to know for certain if some of them joined the Templars.

Disastrous succession issues also afflicted royal families. That
happened in 1290 when the last direct heir to the Scottish crown
passed away. Civil war promptly broke out among the rival
claimants to the throne, and the St. Clairs were caught up in the
fray. One of the claimants was the famous Robert the Bruce. Another was the powerful English king Edward I. So English armies
were soon fighting on Scotland's battlefields.

This warfare came to Roslin in 1303, with Henry St. Clair, the
7th Baron of Roslin, surviving that engagement and bringing home
a respected English prisoner. This gentleman astutely pointed out
that the modest St. Clair castle was highly vulnerable to attack,

but a nearby promontory overlooking the North Esk River would be a vastly superior location. Following that prudent advice, Henry began to build a new Roslin Castle—the one that still stands today.

While that fortification was under construction, Henry learned a most incredible event had occurred. The Knights Templar who had risen to prominence and high esteem all across Europe were suddenly attacked in October of 1307 by the king of France and the pope. Not long thereafter the nearby Templar preceptory at Balantrodoch became abandoned except for two caretaker knights.

Henry St. Clair, living four miles west of Balantrodoch, was of course sympathetic to the plight of his knightly neighbors. More than that, he had a family tradition to uphold. The St. Clairs had a habit of tweaking the powers-that-be and aiding outcasts, as they showed quite clearly when bands of gypsies passed through. For years the St. Clairs hosted these social pariahs on their grounds, which then became the site of considerable festivities. When dour-faced men in Edinburgh objected at this flouting of their laws against aiding gypsies, the St. Clairs eventually gave up those public displays. But then they took other opportunities to aid people downtrodden by higher authorities. It was proudly in their nature.

In any event, during the first month after the Templars were attacked, there was no question Sir Henry would give his neighbors shelter. But then the pope's order arrived that ordered Christians to give no aid to the Templars under pain of excommunication. By this time Robert the Bruce and Scotland were already excommunicated for a prior offence, so that papal directive did not have as much force as it might have had in other days. But even so, after the first few weeks whatever generosity could be given by St. Clair or others in Scotland would have had to be judicious and covert.

So the world into which the fugitive Templars cautiously made their way was torn by pitched battles between Englishmen and Scots. Within a few short years a decisive moment came for Scotland and—some believe—for the Knights Templar and Freemasons. This was the Battle of Bannockburn.

Fig. 18   Roslin Castle

Before the close of the year 1313, all the towns and fortresses of Scotland had yielded to the victorious Bruce with the exception of the Castle of Stirling, and the Governor of this stronghold had entered into an agreement with the Scots to surrender it into their hands if not relieved before the feast of St. John the Baptist in the following year. Edward II and his barons, who were now thoroughly aroused by the extreme urgency of the case, reconciled their differences, and, collecting the whole force of the realm of England, set forth to the relief of the garrison. Robert Bruce on his side was not idle. He ordered a general rendezvous of all the forces of Scotland at the Torwood Forest between Stirling and Falkirk, and not the last to arrive on that classic ground were Sir Henry St. Clair, and his son, Sir William, with the men-at-arms and troops of Roslin. In the celebrated battle which ensued, both these knights greatly distinguished themselves, and for his good services at Bannockburn, and on other occasions, King Robert made Sir Henry a grant of the muir of Pentland and several other lands.[19]

One of the enduring legends of Bannockburn was that when the battle stood in danger of being lost, a force of Knights Templar showed up to aid Scotland and save the day. This would have been a remarkable accomplishment, since the Templar Order had already been disbanded by the pope prior to this time. Presumably these Templars had been in hiding for the intervening years, waiting for the right time to emerge in full uniform and glory. In return for their critical intervention, a grateful King Robert was said to have rewarded the Templar knights by creating Freemasonry. This would have allowed them to continue conducting their affairs with a new outward appearance. Individual people and groups have supported this explanation since at least 1825.

But a contrary view was given by John Barbour in 1375—much closer to the actual events—who saw no Templars in their distinctive uniforms.

Then he [Robert the Bruce] sent all the small folk and camp-followers, and all the harness and victual that were in the Park, a great way from him, and made them leave the field of battle....

At this moment, when the battle was in this fashion being fought, and either side was struggling right manfully, the yeomen, swains, and camp-followers who had been left in the Park to mind the victual, knowing for certain that their lords had joined battle and were in dire conflict with their foes, made one of themselves captain, and fastened broad sheets for banners upon long poles and spears, and said they would see the fight, and help their lords to their utmost. When all were agreed to this, and were come together in a body, they were fifteen thousand and more. Then they hastened forward all in a rout with their banners, like men strong and stout. They came with their whole host to a place where they could see the battle. Then all at once they gave a great shout, "Upon them! On them boldly!" and therewith they all came on.

But they were yet a long way off when the English, who were being driven back by force of battle as I have said, saw coming towards them with a shout a company which seemed full as great as the host they were fighting, and which they had not seen before....

When the King of England saw his men in sundry places flee, and saw the host of his foes become strong and bold, and the English array altogether defeated and without strength to withstand its enemies, he was so vastly dismayed that, with all his company, five hundred armed cap-a-pie, in utter disorder, he took to flight, and made for the castle.[20]

So the sudden appearance of 15,000 reinforcements seemed to carry the day, with no Templars in view. If the Templars were not present in their uniforms to win the battle, then King Robert the

Bruce could not have rewarded them by creating Freemasonry on that day.

But disproving that story does not disprove all possible links between Templars and Masons.

In fact, like most myths, there are sometimes kernels of truth in fantastic accounts such as that one. Sir Henry St. Clair was clearly at the Battle of Bannockburn. And if he gave aid to his fugitive Templar neighbors before they dispersed to parts unknown, which was not only reasonable but almost required for fellow knights, his friendship would not be soon forgotten. When Sir Henry set out for Bannockburn, to put his life on the line for his king, it would not have been unusual for some of the departed Templars to come back quietly, put on Sir Henry's colors, and fight to defend his life in that battle. After the combat, it was not the Templars who were rewarded by the king, it was Sir Henry who received the king's thanks and lands.

But what actually happened behind the scenes in those few days we will never know. The fugitive Templars lived in secrecy at that point because they were outside the law. And the St. Clairs did not violate the trust of their former neighbors by writing about what they knew. So there it remained.

The St. Clair family, on the other hand, went forward with their own lives very publicly. Their stature even moved several steps higher when they added the lands and title of Earl of Orkney to their extensive holdings. To give thanks for all this good fortune the leader of this princely clan set out to build Rosslyn Chapel.

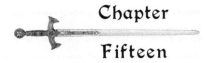

Rosslyn Chapel

When a new William St. Clair took the reins of the family in 1420, he became the 11th Baron of Roslin and 3rd Earl of Orkney. With an impressive castle as his family seat and vast resources flowing to him that could be spent as he willed, Sir William resolved to build a magnificent church unequaled for its beauty in Scotland. He wanted it to not only be his thanks to the Almighty for his good fortune but to provide a final resting place for the bodies of his ancestors and heirs. To do this properly, he wanted four altars for the church, and established a fund to pay four clerics known as canons to pray one after another, twenty-four hours a day, for himself and his ancestors. This required the approval of Pope Eugene IV in Rome, but William had enough influence with the Vatican to request and receive the necessary grant of right for this special place that would become Rosslyn Chapel.

He recruited the best masons he could find and brought them to Roslin around 1441. As their first task, he instructed them to demolish his family's old stone manor house which had long stood on the site. At the same time he gave these masons parcels of land to the northwest of the workplace and allowed them to build homes for themselves using old stones they salvaged from the demolition. These old homes formed the town of Roslin. Several of the residences are still there, though the stones in their walls are chipped and much repaired.

In the course of this work, Sir William directed the masons to remove all of his family's ancient home except for the small chapel at the lowest part of the castle. This modest chapel seemed to possess a special significance to him.

When he received from the pope the formal approval to begin building in 1446, he immediately shifted the masons to construction and the work proceeded quickly. A large foundation was prepared, a cornerstone was laid, and the building began. As the walls started to rise, he had an acknowledgement carved on the exterior north side declaring that Rosslyn Chapel was dedicated in 1450. For decades the work continued under Sir William's supervision, being only a short walk uphill from his castle. With loving attention to each detail, he saw the vastly ornate stonework spread throughout the church.

In the years that followed, Rosslyn Chapel took on an almost mystical quality. It became imbued with legends linking it to Knights Templar, and in fact a new such legend recently emerged. It also became tied to great treasures, grail quests, and the bloodline of Jesus Christ. Further legends joined it to Freemasonry, clandestine rituals, and complex symbology. Still more connected it to pagan practices, sexual orgies, and "green man" icons. Aspects of these legends sound too fantastic to be true, and perhaps they are. But other parts of those legends seem to have a degree of truth, as an exploration of the chapel reveals.

As you approach Rosslyn Chapel there is already a feeling that it is unique. No other building resembles it on the face of the earth. That is partly due to its being incomplete—hewn in two as if a mighty cleaver held by giant hand had come down and severed a cathedral in twain. A massive retaining wall was erected to close off that severed end. Walking closer, the flying buttresses overhead and intricate carvings in the stonework around each stained-glass window presage what is to come.

As you pass under the stone arch of the north doorway and enter the chapel, there is an immediate sense of being surrounded by such a wealth of visual images that the senses are overwhelmed.

Fig. 19   Rosslyn Chapel, just inside the north doorway.
That doorway is seen allowing light to enter from the left.

underneath

Your vision tends to race from delicate carvings close at hand to the soaring ceiling which arches over the rows of pews facing to the east. Turning in that direction and staying close to the left wall, it is necessary to walk upon large floorstones worn smooth with use. No sign reveals that one of the stones underfoot was once the entryway to the burial crypt below.

For generation after generation, the lord and lady of the St. Clairs were laid to rest down there. Each time, the floorstone was lifted and the body was taken below by the few allowed to enter. The mortal remains were placed in the long, east-west underground chamber that reportedly traversed the length of the chapel, but ran southward only to the middle of the church and no farther. The crypt was lined with perfectly-cut ashlar stones, and if there once was a passageway to rooms under the other half of the Chapel, it has not been found. The legendary Holy Grail, Templar treasure, and proof of the bloodline of Jesus Christ have likewise never been found below, though not all are convinced that every possible storage place there has been explored.

The St. Clair men lived their lives so steeped in the honor and duties of knighthood that they refused coffins and other trappings of burial. Instead they insisted upon being placed beneath Rosslyn Chapel clad in full armor. To many, this recalled the exceptional devotion, even unto death, of the Knights Templar. The mystical lore inspired by the rites of the St. Clairs led people to say that the chapel seemed to be awash with flames whenever a St. Clair died. Sir Walter Scott preserved this enchantment in his poetic saga *Lay of the Last Minstrel*.

O'er Roslin all that dreary night
  A wondrous blaze was seen to gleam;
'Twas broader than the watch-fire's light,
  And redder than the bright moonbeam.
It glar'd on Roslin's castled rock,
  It ruddied all the copse-wood glen;
'Twas seen from Dryden's groves of oak
  And seen from cavern'd Hawthornden.
Seem'd all on fire that chapel proud,
  Where Roslin's chiefs uncoffin'd lie,

Each Baron, for a sable shroud,
   Sheath'd in his iron panoply.
Seem'd all on fire within, around,
   Deep sacristy and altar's pale;
Shone every pillar foliage bound,
   And glimmer'd all the dead men's mail.
Blaz'd battlement and pinnet high,
   Blaz'd every rose-carved buttress fair—
So still they blaze when fate is nigh
   The lordly line of high St. Clair.[21]

Returning upward into the passageway above the crypt, and standing on the large floorstones once more, it is possible to continue toward the front of the chapel by passing under a series of arches. These are separated from the body of the church by a row of pillars. Reaching the nave at the eastern end, the four Christian altars requested by William St. Clair are found, each having its own place along the wall. Oddly enough, they are set among detailed carvings that include prominent pagan "green men." In the years before Christianity came to Scotland, the early tribes included in their worship these icons of men's faces with vines and other greenery growing from their mouth. Also included in those pagan devotions were popular practices such as sexual orgies in the springtime. Rituals similar to those pagan rites were alleged to have taken place in the small fields near Roslin Castle at a later date, with the permission and possible participation of the St. Clairs. This echoed the accusations against the Templars of following non-Christian practices.

In the space before the four altars stand the famous three pillars that many people have associated with the three degrees of Masonry: Entered Apprentice, Fellow Craft, and Master. The column that receives the most attention is designated the Apprentice Pillar, and in fact it is the most visually striking. In essence it is a simple fluted column around which four vines seem to grow upward around the pillar from the intricately worked base to an ornate capital. The familiar legend associated with this particular column was that the master carver to whom the pillar was assigned went to Rome before attempting the work so that he could

*Fig. 20   Rosslyn Chapel (a) seen from the north, (b) the three
pillars, (c) ears of corn, (d) ritual scene.*

see the original on which it was to be based. While he was gone, however, an apprentice executed the work brilliantly. When the master returned, he was so outraged at having been upstaged by the apprentice that he killed the young man with a blow from his mallet. A head carved elsewhere in the chapel once showed a mark on the figure's forehead, and it was believed that this was made for the apprentice. It is a beautiful legend. Yet some argue against it being true since there were only two degrees of masons at the time Rosslyn Chapel was built, with a third degree being added only after Grand Lodges were formed several centuries later. However the head of each lodge was called the Master, which was a formally recognized position at that time even though it was not a "degree." It has also been said that the mark on the stone head was not on the original figure, but was added much later to resemble the story—though such an assertion would be difficult to prove one way or the other.

Moving to the south wall of the chapel and looking up, "ears of corn" form an arch over the nearest window. They are somewhat rectangular in design, but could easily be American corn. Many people have suggested that they had to be something else, because Columbus did not "discover" America until after Rosslyn Chapel was already built. Yet it is clear that in the early 1400s Norwegian settlers were already bringing back products from their permanent colonies in Greenland and Iceland as well as their temporary settlements in America. And one of the ports of call on that trade route was the Orkney Islands owned by William St. Clair.

Continuing toward the west along that same wall brings us to a doorway, where something else of interest waits just outside. Stepping through the doorway and then to the right, a stained glass window appears. On the lower left-hand side of the window frame rests a stone corbel carved with an intricate tableau. Of the two men pictured, the one in front has part of his clothing removed, and a rope known as a cable-tow is circled around his neck. This ritual is familiar to every Freemason, since each person participates in it before becoming a Mason. Considering the several details present in the image, the whole scene matches no currently known ritual or practice in the world other than Freemasonry. The images have become worn with time, but observers in previous years recorded that the man standing in back had a large Templar cross on the front of his uniform. This would suggest that it was not a Masonic ritual being shown, but a Knights Templar ritual.

It might be possible that Freemasons were simply imitating the Templars in this regard, except for one thing. I have never met a Mason who knew that the ritual performed with a cable tow was once a Templar ritual. The Masonic ritual continues to be performed this way simply because it has always been done this way, without anyone knowing its origin. Certainly this single observation would not by itself be enough to establish a Templar-Freemason connection. Yet it is worth keeping in mind as other things begin to emerge.

Going back inside the chapel, we then turn right and pass below the corn once again. In front of us, another remarkable sight appears: the Lower Chapel. Amid all the perfection of Rosslyn Chapel's design and crafting, the stairs to the Lower Chapel appear extraordinarily out of place. Located where they are, they required the fourth altar to be placed higher than the other three, since it sits atop the passageway through which the stairs descend. It also left almost no room in front of the altar for the canon to stand and say his prayers. If he stepped back too far from the altar, he fell down the stairwell. What compelling importance did the St. Clairs attach to the Lower Chapel, that they did not allow a single stone to be moved from it—even at the cost of forcing the design of their otherwise magnificent Rosslyn Chapel to be made irregular at this point?

As we descend the steps of the staircase we begin to see the ancient chapel. It is made entirely of stone and comprises only one-fifth the size of the grand edifice above. The amenities in this small space are basic, and it is very simply adorned. The St. Clair cross differed from the traditional cross in that it had many small, semi-circular "bites" taken out of its edges, creating a very distinctive image. The rounded roof of this Lower Chapel still bears the scalloped design drawn from that cross. At the far end of the room stands a simple altar. An impressive stained glass window rises above it, being about nine feet tall. The stone floor extends underfoot roughly 36 feet long and 14 feet wide, meeting the ashlar stone walls on all sides that rise to the curved ceiling above. The feeling of permanence and centuries permeates this solid structure. A modest fireplace rests nearby along the right-hand wall, and a doorway just beyond leads outside. The left-hand wall likewise contains a doorway that once led outside, but was converted long ago to add a small storage or living area. The stonework of this addition is rough-hewn and made of odd-shaped rectangular stones rather than the carefully masoned stone blocks of the original construction and of Rosslyn Chapel above.

What was the importance of this rustic chapel below, that contrasted with the intricately ornate Rosslyn Chapel above? Why were Christian, pagan, Templar and possibly Masonic images placed there? It now appears that Rosslyn Chapel may have been significant to the Templars and Freemasons, but perhaps not in the way we expected.

Several generations after Rosslyn's builder died, one of his descendants made the St. Clair family's link to Freemasonry much clearer. This later William St. Clair became invested as the 19th Baron of Roslin in 1706. Unfortunately the intervening years had not been kind to his family's wealth nor to Rosslyn Chapel. When his ancestors ran out of money to complete their work, the half-done church was sealed off with a wall at what should have been its midpoint. Thereafter, simple maintenance was an expensive chore and the magnificent chapel fell into a state of disrepair. Yet even without funds Sir William was so highly regarded that he stood out among the Masons who gathered at Edinburgh in 1736 to create a Grand Lodge for Scotland. He was their resounding choice to serve as Grand Master. William remained a Freemason thereafter, a time in which Masonry flourished in Scotland.

The members of the St. Clair family thus lived in the world of Templars, stonemasons, Freemasons and knights during tumultuous times. They opened the door to these societies for us, but to see what happened when the fugitive Templars began their rebellious activities we need to probe the world of Freemasons and stonemasons a little further.

Fig. 21   William St. Clair, Grand Master of Scotland

James Mack

How did Freemasonry come into being? Most of the mystery-shrouded activities of that society's early years were so tightly bound and so little shared that they eventually fell from view. Masons commemorate that simple reality in their rituals today by lamenting that the original Master Mason's secrets have been lost, and only a substitute for them remains. The inciting incidents responsible for creating this clandestine society are now no longer consciously known by Masons.

To compensate for this lack of records about their society's early days they launched a veritable cottage industry of creative story-making. In these accounts Freemasonry is frequently associated with Medieval stonemasons. It is also traced back to almost every famous man in history—even to Adam in the Garden of Eden. Masons usually call these stories "traditions" rather than history, as a nod to their questionable nature. Even so, a surprising number of Masons treat many parts of them as being factual.

It became widely believed that the critical connection between Freemasons and stonemasons occurred in a smooth transition over a long period of time. Yet James Mack, Master of the Lodge of Edinburgh (Mary's Chapel) was among those who knew from personal experience what actually happened.

It should first be noted that Freemasons distinguish themselves from working stonemasons by referring to the latter as "operative masons." They then refer to themselves as "speculative masons." Since that proves to be confusing to many people, only the original terms are used here. Men working with stones are known as "stonemasons" or "masons" — and members of the secretive society are "Freemasons" or "Masons."

Looking at what happened in England, we see that the largest group of stonemasons was the Masons Livery Company of London. This clearly was a group of craftsmen in 1481 when King Edward IV granted it the coveted right to wear a distinctive livery uniform and march in the city's formal ceremonies.

However in the 1600s some gentlemen began to be admitted who were not masons by trade. This has often been presented as a gradual change to Freemasonry. Or was it? In 1717 when four Masonic lodges in London came together to form the Grand Lodge, the large and prestigious Masons Livery Company was not one of them. In fact, the Masons Livery Company still exists today, and has never joined the Grand Lodge. It even went a step further and declared on its website that it has no link to Freemasonry. So how does this illustrate a gradual transition to Freemasonry? That is a mystery.

The situation was clearly different in Scotland, where we find records of transitions in some of the lodges. When changes came, however, they seemed to have more to do with sharp drops in membership and natural disasters. A chain of raging fires destroyed much of Edinburgh in the years before 1674, causing the old wooden structures to be largely replaced by buildings made of stone. The demand for new construction became so great that owners no longer required their workers be members of the lodge in Edinburgh. Almost anyone could get work as a mason, and many did. The Lodge of Edinburgh (Mary's Chapel) was one of the largest and most important lodges in Scotland, but now membership fell drastically.

The death knell for this honored working lodge came in 1726. This was nine years after Freemasons in London had already formed their Grand Lodge. And James Mack was active in causing that change.

> In December 1726 one of the members, James Mack, reported that a number of "creditable tradesmen" in the city were anxious to join the Lodge, and were each of them willing to give "a guinea in gold for the use of the poor." The proposed candidates were all men from other trades, and although the golden guineas were very tempting, the diehard operatives in the Lodge rejected the proposal.
>
> A month later Mack returned to the attack, at a meeting which he had apparently called without permission of the Master of the Lodge. The question of the proposed admissions was reopened, and there was a thundering row. The Master and Warden "walked out," and the remaining five proceeded to elect new officers, choosing Mack as "preses" or Master. Three "entered-apprentices" from other lodges, *all non-operative*, were admitted and passed F.C.; and seven burgesses, *none of them masons*, were received "entered apprentices and fellow crafts." In February 1727 another eight non-operatives were admitted, and the operative character of the Lodge was completely lost. The extent of the change may be judged from the fact that in 1736, when the Lodge compiled its first complete code of By-laws, not a single regulation was made which concerned the mason trade. The transition was virtually complete![22]

In other words, this was not the gradual, evolutionary change evoked by the term "smooth transition." It was more consistent with the term *coup d'état*, in which new people abruptly took over the prior organization and put it to new use.

With the Lodge of Edinburgh being an ancient "flagship" of stonemasonry in Scotland, the other stonemason lodges eventually followed its course, without the need for an explosive meeting.

They either brought in many members from outside masonry, or closed their doors and went out of existence.

So the easy route of assuming that stonemasons' lodges made a gradual transition to Freemasons' lodges has not turned out to match the actual events. How did Freemasonry develop? And what happened during those secretive early years?

Clues abound in the tumultuous years after the Templars were attacked, as their fugitive members began to make their way forward.

Brothers Emerge

Sir Walter de Clifton and his fellow knights among the Templars came from some of the most noble families of Europe. When he and those other knightly sons were charged with heresy in 1307—and hundreds of them were put to death—the anger in those noble families was difficult to contain. Yet contain it they did, for the king had ordered this, and the pope affirmed it. Those were powers that could not be challenged.

But these families, indirectly attacked in this way, could still care for their sons. When the trials ended and the slain were mourned, the surviving knights slowly began to emerge from the covert houses in which they had taken refuge.

Their families could not welcome them openly and risk the wrath of king and church, but they could help quietly—restoring their sons to some semblance of their former life. It took only a reasonable estate with a proper manor house, and fields to support it, to bring each knight back to something resembling a normal life. After he adopted a new name and registered his property, he was well on the way to taking a significant place in society again. No longer bound by the restrictions of celibacy, the former knight was free to take a wife. And when he sired children he was able to teach them the lessons learned during a difficult and tumultuous life. One of those lessons was the value of close brotherhood like the one that had saved his life. For him to return to the lodging house where he lived during the most difficult years of his life was a natural step, along with feeling a strong need to respond to brothers in distress—even as he had once been in need himself, and received that relief.

Clerical brothers among the Templars likewise folded their green robes for the last time, laid them down, and went to live in that underground world. They took with them a high degree of literacy and whatever level of skill in finance, commerce and legal matters they had developed while in the Order. Upon the cessation of their brothers' trials and tribulations, these men had to move on, just as their knightly brothers had done. Yet a different world awaited them.

There were no rich family members to embrace them, nor were fertile estates given to them. Yet they were not without strengths of their own. The monetary, legal and organizational skills that enabled them to build and operate one of the greatest financial systems in the world were still with them. Using a covert piece of former Templar property as collateral, or imposing upon a noble brother for such a lien, they were soon back in business again—serving as a trader, builder, financial provider or practitioner of the law.

These former clerics no longer needed to send the earnings of their labor to battlefields in the East to be consumed in the fire of warfare. Their profits stayed with them and multiplied in their well-trained hands. Mindful of the dark days when they needed shelter, and received the assistance of Templar brothers, they were likewise be unable to refuse requests for help. Employing their former servingmen or clerical brothers when asked, or providing professional assistance to noble brothers when needed, their life went on. The clandestine lodging places they once occupied were not forgotten. Returning to spend an occasional evening with former brothers sufficed to keep the memory alive. Like their knightly brethren, they were also able to take a wife and give themselves children to carry on their name and their small but

growing fortunes. How much they told their children about the
life they had lived depended on each man. But the lessons they
learned—the brotherhood, the wariness of unlimited church or
state power, and the blessings of literacy—these they could pass
on to their children with an urgency their children might not un-
derstand.

Since some of these former Templars practiced law, it is interesting that when the Templar preceptory in London was seized by
the king after 1307, it was recorded that a number of practitioners
of the law were in residence there, and claimed to hold leases. The
preceptory property passed through several hands thereafter, but
it was always leased to these barristers. In due course the property
was deeded to the barristers' legal associations and became two of
the Inns of Court—known as Inner Temple and Middle Temple.
These barristers still occupy the Templar grounds and buildings
today. It has never been determined whether those original practitioners of the law who created this legacy once wore green robes.

The servingmen of the Templar Order did not have the same
bountiful opportunities accorded to knights and clerics. They had
lived the life of tradesmen and assistants, earning their room and
board with the skill of their hands and the sweat of their brow.
But they had also learned discipline and the same high standards
as the knights and clerks who considered themselves among the
best in the world at what they did. That was a thing of value. And
they had experienced something that was both wonderful and
terrible: though they came from mean circumstances, they had
been treated like brothers by men of noble blood and high education. It was difficult for them to face going back to being a piece of
chattel on a rich man's property, a condition that afflicted most of
their peers in those days.

So when they no longer had to live in hiding and could go out
into society as their own man, they did so with some amount of
concern. A few did not have to venture out at all, staying on as
innkeepers in the old lodgings. There they were able to host the
private gatherings of their brothers—the men who had once been
Templars. Those who stepped out into the world of course made
their first request for employment to the former knights and

*Fig. 22   This original Templar buttery hall is still used by the
barristers in London*

clerics of their Order, who could not refuse them. The former serv-ingmen had skill maintaining estates, assisting gentlemen, and performing trades such as masonry and carpentry. These were all valuable services that helped their more fortunate brothers sustain their properties and holdings. When they had their feet under them, these working brothers then moved on to higher positions, or went into their own trade as a master.

For almost two hundred years the Knights Templar had been renowned for their unquestioned devotion to God, courage, secre-cy, financial prowess, discipline and unity. It was intended to be a good preparation for battle. It also turned out to be a good prepa-ration for life.

Yet just as they fondly remembered the brotherhood once shared as Templars, they also remembered the deaths of their brothers and their own outcast status without any fondness at all. Their rebellion against that treatment began on the same day they be-came fugitives and moved into secret residences in defiance of the king's law and the church's commands. They adopted new names, wore new clothes and created new modes of recognition to identi-fy themselves to fellow conspirators. At first it was simply done to survive the warrants against them. But these were acts of rebellion and would be punished as such.

It grew from there. They owed their escape and survival to the brothers who stood by them, but they were so few against so many. And now they had families to protect as well. So they care-fully accepted new members.

All around them men and their families were being driven from hearth and home by excessive taxation, onerous laws, Inqui-sition and charges of heresy. They saw in those outcasts mirror images of themselves. So they began to hold out their hand to worthy men among these fugitives, taking them into the shelter of this growing organization.

And as they brought new brothers into the fold, the nature of their actions against the power of kings and the Vatican began to change.

"Peasants Revolt
1381

Wat Tyler

Wat Tyler had suffered at the church's hand and was not about to accept it quietly. Even so it was a strange set of circumstances that made him the leader of the Peasants' Revolt in England during 1381. He knew the quiet society to which he belonged was taking a great risk by venturing this far out into public view. Yet here he stood at the head of over one hundred thousand people in open revolt. Following his lead these rebels stormed across the countryside into London, burning down palatial manors along the way.

Nor was he acting alone. As Wat and this followers marched and rampaged, word gradually seeped out that the spreading rebellion was guided by a Great Society. This revolt was so remarkable that hundreds of years later a man named Winston Churchill was moved to note, "Throughout the summer of 1381 there was a general ferment. Beneath it all lay organization. Agents moved round the villages of central England, in touch with a 'Great Society' which was said to meet in London."[23]

Adding to the strangeness of this actions was that Wat and his followers displayed an especially strong distaste for the Knights Hospitaller—the rival of the Templars.

All of the religious orders owned properties in London, but only the Hospitaller property was deliberately sought out for destruction, and not just the major establishments at St John's Clerkenwell, and the "Temple" area between Fleet Street and the Thames. The chroniclers state that the rebels sought out every Hospitaller house and rental property to smash or burn it....

In all of the destruction in London, why did the rebels not burn the records stored in the Hospitaller church off Fleet Street right where they found them? Why go to all the trouble of carrying boxes and bundles out of the church to the high road, away from the building, unless it was to avoid the risk of damage to the structure? How was this church different from any other property? Only in that it had been the principal church in Britain of the Knights Templar, consecrated almost three hundred years earlier, in 1185, by Heraclius, the patriarch of Jerusalem. The manner of its consecration alone didn't set it apart, however, because the patriarch had also consecrated the Hospitaller church at Clerkenwell in 1185, during the same month that he had dedicated the Templar church; yet no consideration was given by the rebels to protecting the church at Clerkenwell.[24]

Historian John Robinson pointed out that Pope Clement had not only dissolved the Knights Templar but ordered all their property be given to the Hospitallers. So he concluded that the organization behind this revolt was descended from the Templars, and still bore animosity toward the Hospitallers. It turns out he was right about the first part. The animosity, if it still existed, was secondary.

Wat Tyler and his followers did not just destroy Hospitaller property. They made a special point of finding the records held in each place and burning them. The Templar property acquired by the Hospitallers had included the records of estates and personnel, to the extent that those records escaped destruction on the days the Templars fled. These documents hung like a sword over the heads of the escaped Templars and their heirs. The pope's charges of heresy and orders of excommunication against them had never been revoked. Penalties or social stain would still fall upon the families of former Templars if those records were ever released. When the records were taken out of the Hospitaller properties—and especially out of Temple Church—and then burned, that threat was permanently erased.

Wat clearly knew the individuals and society from whom he received guidance. But most of the people in the Peasants' Revolt had little knowledge of this Great Society. Nor should it be expected that this was the society's real name. If those unseen sponsors were conducting their affairs secretly, as they clearly were, they would not parade their identity in public but rather use another name for that purpose. The "Great Society" label existed only during this revolt and not thereafter.

The rank-and-file people who marched in this revolution and burned those buildings were not armchair conspirators. They by and large were simple folk who joined the revolt because they tilled the land and worked their crafts under the difficult burden of oppressive laws. Their anger and passions were primed and ready to break lose in wanton rioting, looting and destruction. What made this revolt surprisingly different from the riotous behavior of most others was how much it remained under control. Wat and his secretive brothers who formed the leadership kept everyone in order, targeting some individuals and specific places for destruction while sparing others. There were highly coordinated activities in many different cities.

> ....Messengers came into Cambridgeshire from London and from John Wrawe in Suffolk, both reporting high levels of success and urging the locals to rise. On June 14 the first rebel attack in Cambridgeshire singled out a manor of the Knights Hospitaller at Chippenham. The next day the revolt exploded at a dozen different places throughout the county. Men rode through the county announcing that serfdom had ended. One man, Adam Clymme, ordered that no

Fig. 23   The Peasants Revolt of 1381

man, whether bound or free, should obey any lord or perform any services for him, upon pain of beheading, unless otherwise ordered by the Great Society....[25]

John Robinson saw these organizers as remnants of the Knights Templar, but he also noted another "secret society" that seemed to exist in England at that time, and this was Freemasonry. If Masonry did exist then, was there any connection between it and this revolt, or with the Templars? He made some interesting discoveries.

Although Freemasonry was a secret society before 1717, much of its practices, rituals and symbols have come into public view since then. Even so, it turned out that many words, symbols and practices used by Freemasons in lodge rituals had no real meaning in English. They were simply passed from older brothers to younger brothers just as they were, because the ritual included them that way. Yet these things must have had some meaning hundreds of years ago in Masonry's early days.

From his background in Medieval studies, Robinson was aware that Hugh de Payens and a large number of Templar knights were from France. French was also the official language used in English courts until 1362, a holdover from the Norman conquest of England by William the Conqueror. So could the explanation for some words in Freemasonry be found in Medieval French?

One of the mysteries he addressed was the name of the central figure in the Masonic Third Degree initiation ritual, Hiram Abiff. This man was described in the Bible as the master builder of Solomon's Temple, and was known simply as Hiram with no last name. Yet in Masonic lore he was always called Hiram Abiff and was identified by the initials H.A. or H.A.B. This path did not look promising when there turned out to be no Medieval French word corresponding to "abiff." But the reference in some sources to H.A.B. was intriguing. It would only be written that way if the name had originally been in three parts, as in Hiram A. Biff. In French the word "biffer" meant "to strike out or eliminate." In Masonic tradition, Hiram is struck upon the head with a mallet and killed. So "Hiram à biffe" or "Hiram who was struck and eliminated" apparently became his identifying name. Over the hundreds of years that this name was passed down in oral tradition, the original meaning had been lost and Masons simply repeated and wrote what they heard, which was Hiram Abiff.

If that had been the only puzzling Masonic expression which made sense in Medieval French, it would simply have been interesting and "maybe" true. But this was just the first of many cases where Medieval French, the language of the Templars, was the key that opened a lock, as we will see.

Medieval French

White Lambskin
About Their Loins

Imagine that you are an Entered Apprentice in an early Masonic lodge and about to attend one of its secret meetings. Being an Entered Apprentice means you have just become a Mason—so you are allowed to attend the meetings, but do not really know what is going on yet. This is in keeping with the Masonic custom of letting things slowly seep in over time—you learn by degrees. As you approach the lodge-room door, there is a man barring the way. He wears a medallion with the symbol of a drawn sword.

The Templars also placed an officer at the door during their secret meetings. But that man carried an actual sword, drawn and ready for use. The similarity between these two customs is striking. It is a practice unlike anything that occurs in stonemasonry or virtually any other society.

That could mean Masons were simply imitating the Templars—if it was not for the peculiar name of this officer. Masons call him the Tyler. Yet if you ask him why he has this name, he does not really know. Most Masons hazard a guess that it has something to do with stonemasonry. In fact there was a "tiler" who set tiles. But that kind of tiler had nothing to do with guarding doors, or even making doors.

On the other hand if we look into the Medieval French spoken by Templars, we see the word *tailleur* meant "the one who cuts." The cloth-cutter came down to us with the name *tailor*. In similar fashion, the man at the door who cuts with his sword has come down to us as *tyler*. The French word fits the insignia and function of this officer in Freemasonry.

If the Tyler knows you, the door is opened. If not, he asks a series of questions you must answer to show you are a Mason. When he is satisfied, the door opens and you go in.

Upon entering a lodge meeting that is already in session, you must give what is called the "due guard," a formal sign of recognition. This is another term that has no real meaning in English. But if we look back into Medieval French, it is an expression that once had clear meaning. In those days the traditional term for a knight or soldier's protective gesture was "gest du garde." This became shortened in usage to "du garde." English-speaking people heard these words, repeated them, then began to write them as "due guard" in Masonic usage. Once again, it referred to a knightly practice rather than some other training.

These words in Medieval French point to a link between Masonry and the Templars in the 1300s, when French was still the language of courts and gentlemen in England. In fact Masonry has a number of words and practices that its members repeat without really knowing the original meaning. That is a good thing, because it makes Masonry like a time machine into which things from long ago were placed and preserved for us to see today.

As you stand in the lodge room where the meeting is going on, if you did not put on a Masonic apron before you entered, you must put one on now. Entered Apprentices are eligible to wear a simple cloth apron of Masonic design. But when you complete the Third Degree ritual and become a Master Mason, you receive the ultimate adornment of a Mason and that is the apron made of pure white lambskin. It is a truly memorable moment.

That apron has long been considered one of the clearest links to stonemasons of old. The reality, however, is somewhat different. No records have been found showing a stonemason wearing an apron of expensive white lambskin. Such work apparel would have been destroyed during the first day on the job by dirt and gashes from rough pieces of stone. Stonemasons wore clothing of sterner stuff. Who, then, wore white lambskin aprons?

The written Rule of the Knights Templar set a requirement of chastity within the Order. To help brothers keep this vow it required them to wear a girding garment of white lambskin around their loins at all times. This was not taken off for any reason, even for bathing. For that reason it became a distinguishing mark of the Templars by which they identified their brothers. This was a custom not generally seen or known to the public. For that reason there was no public catch-phrase or emulation of "wearing lambskin like a Templar." Much like the words in French repeated by people after the original meaning was lost, the wearing of white lambskin "aprons" was done by Masons for one reason only: because it had always been done. So the tradition continued.

In many Masonic lodges, particularly in Great Britain, the wearing of gloves is also traditional. In 1686 Robert Plot described a ceremony in which Freemasons were presented with gloves by new brothers coming into Masonry. So this was a longstanding custom. Going back a step further, we saw that the clerics of the Knights Templar, in addition to their green robes with the red Templar cross, also wore gloves in the performance of their duties.

While this obligatory practice of hand covering applied to all priests among the Templars, in most other religious groups the wearing of gloves was extremely rare. It was generally limited to bishops and higher prelates. It was a distinction and honor cherished by the Templar clergy. These clerical brothers were well positioned to be among the surviving Templars, since they were responsible for the safe houses in which the Templars took refuge. Gloves were a small, inconspicuous thing they could bring with them as a reminder of brighter Templar days.

Once again standing in the lodge room, as you look around you see one symbol displayed more prominently than any other. That is the square and compass, the image by which Masonry is recognized all over the world.

Trying to track the origin of that symbol, Robinson noted that—like most people on the run from authorities—fugitive Templars had to meet in isolated forests and temporary rooms. They needed to bring with them everything required for their ceremonies, then go away as quietly as they came. In case they were stopped by the authorities—which was a frequent occurrence in those days of runaway serfs, highwaymen and other fugitives from the law—the covert Templars could not be carrying obvious symbols of a secret society. That would lead to immediate arrest and whatever punishment local authorities chose to dole out. So the things these conspirators used in their ceremonies had to be items of innocent appearance—until they were properly brought together during the secret rites.

Today, Masonic oaths are normally taken on a Bible, with a compass and square resting on top of it. This is different than the Templar oaths, which were taken on a Bible with a cross depicted on the front, like the one Sir Walter described at his trial. Those Templar Bibles were written by hand and were in Latin, as were all the other Bibles of that day. In addition, those hand-copied Latin Bibles were primarily kept in churches. So any secret society related to the suppressed Templars had to use some other symbol in place of a Bible during the oath-taking.

Robinson found a related symbol that was surprisingly good. The Poor Fellow-Soldiers of Christ and the Temple of Solomon were of course familiar with the Seal of Solomon, the symbol used by one of their principal benefactors. This seal resembled the six-pointed Star of David, except that it was made of two triangles, one white and one black. It would have been instantly recognizable to all of their brothers. In fact an old Templar medallion found in France showed exactly that. It consisted of a circle within which were inscribed two equilateral triangles placed one on top of the other, so as to form a six-pointed star. In the center of the star was a second circle, containing inside it the lamb of the order of the Temple holding a banner in its fore-paw.

Yet carrying symbols that resembled the Jewish Star of David in staunchly Catholic Europe at that time would have been a severe problem. It could have easily led to that undesired arrest by the authorities of church and state. However, if one simply dropped the two horizontal lines from the Seal of Solomon, an immediately recognizable design was formed—that of a square and compass.

Sq | Compass

Fig. 24   Seal of Solomon, showing square and compass

Men could then go to their meetings carrying a square and compass without arousing any suspicion. If stopped by authorities of the king or church, they could simply say, "I am a mason," and go on. In addition, stonemasons were not like serfs or local craftsmen who were confined to the estate on which they were born. As masons, the brothers could travel in their own country and in foreign lands. The compass and square they carried were their passport, requiring only a local mason as a character witness.

This custom of traveling masons became so well established in Europe that even in the late 1600s Freemason Sir Robert Moray used it to gain the right to be in the Netherlands. Moray went to live in that country for a period of time, and in the local archives the following entry was recorded by the authorities.

> On the 10th of March, 1659, appeared Sir Robert Moray, Knight, born in Scotland, Privy Councillor of the King of Great Britain in Scotland, and Colonel of the Scottish Guards in the service of His Majesty, the King of France, aged fifty years, presented by Everard, master of the Craft of masons. He took under this craft the necessary oath, and the right of citizenship was granted him, according to custom. [26]

Many pieces of evidence have brought Masonry closer to the Knights Templar: the square and compass symbol, aprons, gloves and numerous ancient words. Yet as persuasive as this evidence seemed to be in 1989 when Robinson introduced most of these points, the debate over a connection between Templars and Masons continued.

Fortunately some additional, intriguing pieces of information have come to light. They yield revealing clues not only to Masonry's relationship with the Knights Templar, but on the Templar rebellion against excessive power wielded by kings and popes. Let us unroll some actual manuscripts from Medieval and later times that fill in some pieces of this jigsaw puzzle and bring us closer to seeing the whole picture.

Matthew Cooke

Many people were involved in discovering the parchment documents from Masonry's early years that are known as the Old Charges. Those records form a line of 120 manuscripts from the 1300s to 1717 when Freemasonry emerged from secrecy into public view. Each was copied from an earlier parchment, sometimes with a change or two, so that the content gradually evolved over the centuries. These documents described how a person would be "charged" in Masonry to follow good rules in life. Each was couched in the language of stonemasons, but was good advice for anyone.

In England I obtained permission to examine many of these ancient manuscripts and discovered that they filled some significant gaps in the picture of Masonry's relationship with Templars and stonemasons. Just like Masonic ritual, they served to some degree as time capsules that preserved elements of people's lives and what was happening at the time they were written.

Matthew Cooke came across one of the earliest of these and translated it from Old English into modern English, so it is known as the Cooke Manuscript in his honor. This parchment document

Fig. 25   Old Charges manuscripts

was written around the year 1450, and appeared to be copied from an even older manuscript.

It opened with a prayer, which was significant, but even more interesting was the form this prayer took.

> Thanked be God, our glorious Father, the founder and creator of heaven and earth, and of all things that therein are, for that he has vouchsafed, of his glorious Godhead, to make so many things of manifold virtue for the use of mankind....

The more traditional beginning would have acknowledged a temporal authority such as a king or lord, but that was not a requirement. Beginning with a prayer suggests that the group by which this was written had some stronger than normal religious commitment. Yet the strangest part may be what was not said. The Catholic Church was still the dominant religion of Europe in this time before the Protestant Reformation—but after acknowledging God, neither the church nor the pope was mentioned anywhere in the document.

That curious combination calls to mind the unusual requirement made of each person seeking to enter Freemasonry. Before becoming an Entered Apprentice, they had to profess a belief in God. Yet they were not asked, and did not have to declare, a belief in any one particular religion. That was a highly unusual combination, to say the least. Most organizations avoided this difficult subject by making no requirement that a person believe in God. Those groups that did have such a requirement normally went a step further and required a belief in Catholicism, or some other specific doctrine. Masonry did not. So while the Cooke Manuscript prayer would be odd for most other groups, it was a perfect fit with the practices of Freemasons.

On the other hand it was not a good fit for stonemasons. Like most of Europe, Great Britain in the 1400s was almost 100 percent Catholic, with a small number of Jews and people of other faiths. In addition, stonemasons earned a large part of their living by building churches and cathedrals, so their employers were devout members of that same faith. There was no benefit for stonemasons

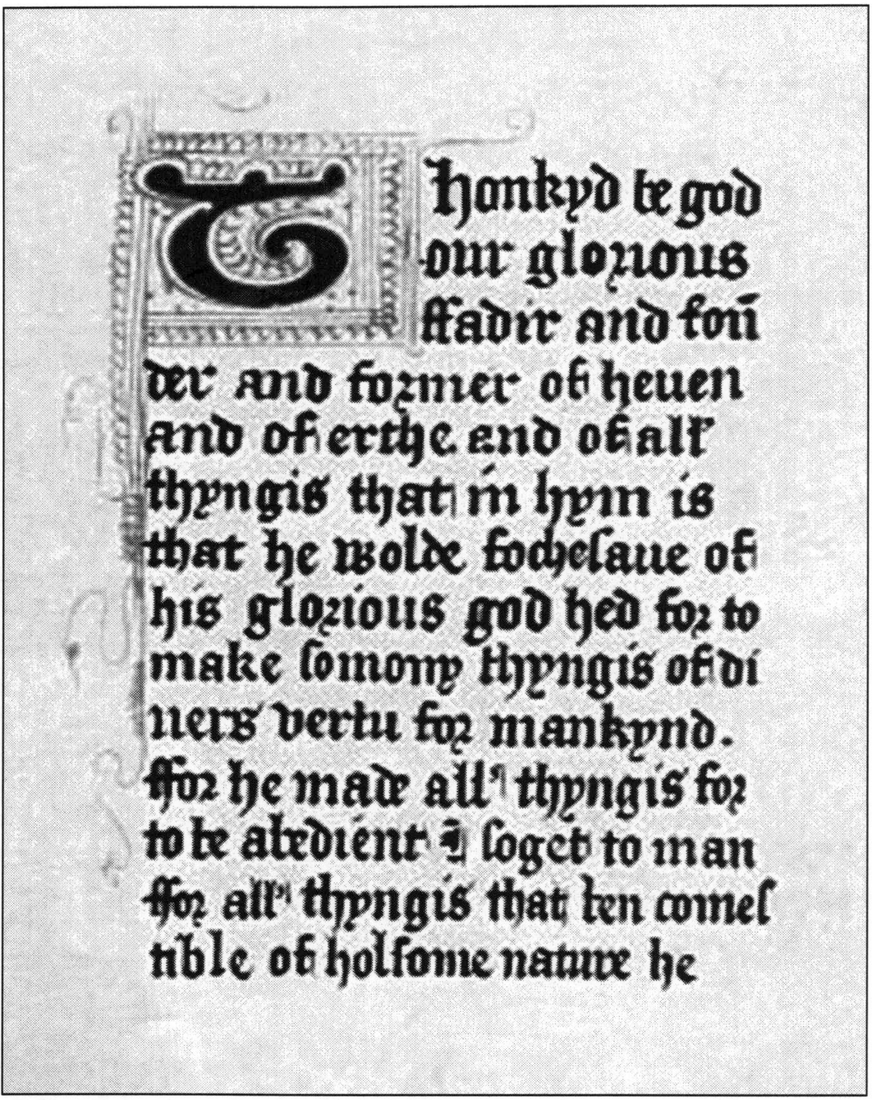

Thonkyd be god
our glorious
ffadir and foũ
der and former of heuen
and of erthe and of all
thyngis that in hym is
that he wolde fochesaue of
his glorious god hed for to
make somony thyngis of di
uers vertu for mankynd.
ffor he made all thyngis for
to be abedient & soget to man
ffor all thyngis that ben comes
tible of holsome nature he

Fig. 26 Cooke Manuscript

to be anything other than staunchly Catholic at that time. In fact, any lack of enthusiasm in that regard could be punishable by inquisition and death, as many in Europe had already discovered. A document of guidelines for stonemasons could easily have avoided mention of religion at all—just as the charters granted by towns to stonemasons often did. Or such a manuscript could bless God and the pope, as was common for documents mentioning religion. It was unnecessary for stonemasons to put their neck on the chopping block by invoking God but not the church or the pope. This by itself would not be sufficient proof that the manuscripts were not created by stonemasons, but it raises reasonable questions.

The Knights Templar, on the other hand, had lived their life deeply connected not only to the service of God, but tied to the pope in every way. The Grand Master of their Order reported directly to the pope, and only to him. So from that standpoint, they also would seem ill-suited to be associated with the Old Charges manuscripts. Of course we now know that was not their whole story.

In 1307 the pope abandoned them, giving them up to be arrested, tortured, and then burned alive. Understandably, that lessened their attachment to the pope. This left the surviving Templars deeply conflicted. They had dedicated their lives to God's service, and the testimony of captured Templars showed that they still felt strongly compelled in that direction. Yet the brothers were understandably split on how to view the religion to which they belonged. That they would create a legacy of love for God—yet omit any reference to the church or the pope from their writings—was fully consistent with their difficult situation.

The next part of Cooke—and usually in other Old Charges as well—was a clear appreciation of the seven arts and sciences, along with a description of them. These were grammar, rhetoric, logic, arithmetic, geometry, music and astronomy. Of them, geometry was given special attention.

In those days a university education was built around the arts and sciences, but with a particular purpose in mind. That purpose was to train new priests and other clergy, with a smaller number of the nobility receiving some part of that education. It was common for kings and lords to require clergy be present at official events to record whatever was necessary, since most of the highly-born people could not write themselves.

Recall for a moment the typical stonemasons' lodge. Standing around blocks of stone upon which they worked, these were rough-handed, unschooled, and largely or completely illiterate men. Now try to imagine them sitting down and attempting to write a document that went into something they never had, and never would have: a university education. And try to imagine these working men putting themselves through all that just to introduce the subject of geometry.

If they hired a scribe to write down their words, and spoke from their own experience, it would have resulted in a far different discussion. That would have produced an interesting document based on the precise squaring of stones, the careful matching of uniquely-shaped columns and arches, and the art of carving which causes faces and flowers to emerge from previously shapeless blocks of stone. At the city of York I talked with a number of stonemasons who still practiced this ancient trade. They spoke of the love they felt for their work, and I learned that they have their own expressions and view of the world. None of that springs from the pages of these manuscripts. An entirely different hand and mind seems to have created them.

On the other hand Freemasons had a close relationship with the arts and sciences. This was perhaps clearest in the rite of the Second Degree that involved the Winding Staircase. Each of the seven arts and sciences was an essential step in the staircase. The connection between Freemasonry and the invoking of the seven arts and sciences in the Old Charges is quite clear.

Among the Knights Templar, the only group that had a close connection with the arts and sciences was the green-robed clerics. These men were well-educated, just like the other clergy of their day. Their experience made them highly skilled in languages of the East and the West, and they were sufficiently capable with numbers to create and maintain the Templar financial institution that spread from Europe to the Middle East.

Given the important role education played in building their financial empire, the Templar survivors would reasonably have given more attention to the seven arts and sciences than the average family that inherited its power and position. All of this was consistent with the discussion in the Old Charges manuscripts.

But there was more to be found in Cooke.

Lost Years, Missing Symbols

$\mathcal{T}$ he Cooke Manuscript went on to recite a "traditional" history of Masonry. This could have been highly revelatory. Unfortunately the attempts made to confirm its content have only revealed this to be fanciful construction. Masons acknowledge that simple fact by calling these accounts "traditions" rather than history. Consider what was done to this verse from the Bible.

> And Adah bare Jabal: he was the father of such as dwell in tents, and of such as have cattle. And his brother's name was Jubal: he was the father of all such as handle the harp and organ.
>
> *Genesis 4:20-21*

In its place the following "tradition" was inserted into Cooke. It showed Masonry magically appearing in these years right after Adam was in the Garden of Eden.

> The elder son Jabal was the first man that ever discovered geometry and masonry, and he made houses, and is called in the Bible the father of all men who

dwell in tents or dwelling houses. And he was Cain's master mason and governor of the works when he built the city of Enoch, which was the first city ever made and was built by Cain, Adam's son, who gave it to his own son Enoch, and give the city the name of his son and called it Enoch, and now it is known as Ephraim. And at that place was the Science of Geometry and Masonry first prosecuted and contrived as a science and as a handicraft.

After the time of Adam, the rest of the tradition wended its way through the work of Euclid in Egypt, Solomon's Temple, Medieval France, and finally England. Its fanciful creations sketched mythological images far removed from reality, capturing a person's imagination the way Greek mythology had once been wont to do.

One reason to create such a mythology would be to fill a blank spot for people who had no idea of their actual history. A second reason would be to help people conceal a history they did not want to come to light. Stonemasons might have fit into the first explanation, since they were not well-educated in history. Freemasons might fit either the first or second explanation. Templar survivors would clearly fall into the second explanation, being fugitives from the law.

These traditions are interesting, but let us go a little further and discover what Templars and Masons were actually doing.

The listed "charges" in the Old Charges were guides to good moral conduct. They were the things each person was "charged" to do in living a good life. These were presented as if said to a stonemason, yet were good allegories for anyone on how to live an honorable life. Freemasons have continued to use this same process for many centuries. The first article in Cooke shows how this worked.

The first article is this. That every master of this art should be wise, and true to the lord who employs him, expending his goods carefully as he would his own were expended; and not give more pay to any mason

than he knows him to have earned, according to the
dearth [or scarcity and therefore price] of corn and
victuals in the country and this without favouritism,
for every man is to be rewarded according to his
work.

The stonemasons of that day could have lived according to
such rules, and may in fact have done so. There were nine articles
and nine points in these charges, and they could have easily been
passed down verbally from masters to apprentices. They were
short enough to be easily memorized and followed, so stonemasons had no need to write them down—even if they had known
how to write. In any event, memorization would have been the
best way to keep these charges on stonemasons' minds every day
in the workplace. They had little need and less ability to pass any
charges along in written form.

For Freemasons, these charges are reflected in rites still being
used today. In the Entered Apprentice degree, when a new Mason
is charged to properly use a twenty-four inch gauge or ruler, he is
actually being urged to divide his twenty-four hour day properly
to meet all his obligations.

This was much like the popular sayings in Benjamin Franklin's
Poor Richard's Almanack, where good advice was dressed in other
clothes. The *Almanack's* expression "a stitch in time saves nine"
clearly had meaning beyond sewing—it offered practical advice
for life. Freemasons used the charges, the tools, and the lodges of
stonemasons as a way to look inside life, and find a better way to
live in society. The Old Charges manuscripts appear to have
served that same role.

A guide to good behavior in society would have been as attractive to survivors of the Knights Templar as it would have been to
any other conscientious member of society. Yet for them, the ap-
plicability of the Cooke Manuscript went a step farther. Just before
the "charges" were listed, a story was told that these guidelines
were needed because of unidentified defects among stonemasons
around 930 AD. The story may or may not be true, but the choice
of words was quite intriguing.

> ...in the time of king Athelstan, sometime king of Eng-
> land, by common assent of his Council and other great
> lords of the land on account of great defects found
> amongst masons, a certain rule was ordained for
> them.

Monastic orders were governed in those days by a Rule. That was the primary use of the term when expressed in this manner. The word "ordained" could mean "ordered" but was most closely associated with religious usage, as in "the novice was ordained into the clergy." Stonemasons were not a religious order. As such, they were not ordained, and did not receive a Rule from the church. It is possible that this was simply a colorful reference, but it would be a highly unusual reference for a stonemason to make about his own occupation. On the other hand, it would be a term familiar to the descendants of a religious brother such as a Knight Templar, whose family had been deeply marked by that experience.

Earlier we saw the possibility of Freemasonry evolving from Medieval stonemason lodges had serious problems, which rendered that path unlikely. The Cooke Manuscript has shown us additional problems in that regard. This poses a dilemma, because the tools and practices of stonemasons were chosen for use in the allegories and symbols of Freemasonry.

Yet in examining many collections of Masonic symbols for clues, I discovered something quite interesting.

The symbols of Freemasonry contain many references to ancient works. The Great Pyramid is portrayed, often with the all-seeing eye. Solomon's Temple appears frequently, including its specific details such as the winding staircase and the twin pillars *Jachin* and *Boaz*. Arches were used in Mesopotamian times and became highly popular among the ancient Romans. The tools of compass, square, plumb and level were also known and used in antiquity.

Yet oddly enough, there are no significant symbols in Masonry relating to Medieval buildings, not even cathedrals. This is true even though those were the main products and hallmarks of Medieval stonemasons. There is no depiction of Notre Dame Cathedral, Westminster Abbey, or other prominent church. There are no church towers in general, nor naves or flying buttresses.

The Masonic symbols that constitute the core of Freemasonry indicate that the connection with stonemasons did not take place during the Medieval period. Instead they show connections to stonemasonry as it existed in ancient times.

Following that thread causes us to look again at the green-robed clerics among the Knights Templar. The Lebanese Christians in this group clung strongly to their Phoenician roots, as many Lebanese people still do today. Their Phoenician forebears had been present at the building of the Great Pyramid, and provided Hiram Abiff along with other masons for the raising of Solomon's Temple. That gave the Knights Templar their strongest link back to the temple for which they were named. It is a link that would have been cherished and remembered.

We saw the fugitive Templars become rebelling knights who refused to submit as ordered by kings and the pope. And when the time came to choose a new name for themselves, a common name so that they could pass without being arrested, the full body of evidence shows they chose to be called Masons. In doing this they chose as their symbols things that would remind them of their past.

At the end of the Cooke Manuscript came the words, "Amen, so mote it be." This was done as if one were closing a prayer. Even today, Freemasons end each prayer with the word "Amen"—to which the brothers respond, "So mote it be." The connection of Old Charges manuscripts to Freemasonry is absolute and clear.

The Cooke Manuscript has opened an interesting look into the lives and practices of this unusual group of people in Britain around the year 1450. To discover more about the early days of this secretive society, let us step back further in time, to see what happened in the 1300s when the Templars were being disbanded.

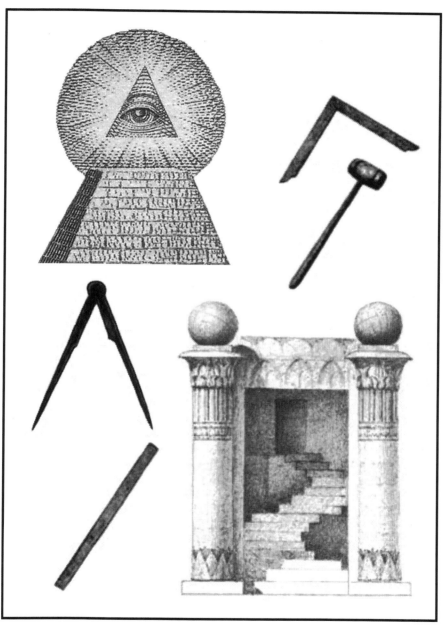

Fig. 27 Symbols of Freemasonry

Regius Manuscript

This search for what the Templars did after leaving their Order comes at last to a manuscript older than Cooke. This is the Regius Manuscript written about 1390, which referred to a related document earlier in the 1300s. Regius was the only Old Charge written as a poem, and it described the people and events one would find in a gentleman's household. This is how it opened.

> Here begin the constitutions of the art
> of Geometry according to Euclid.
>
> Whoever will both well read and look
> He may find written in old book
> Of great lords and also ladies,
> That had many children together, certainly;
> And had no income to keep them with,
> Neither in town nor field nor enclosed wood;
> A council together they could them take,
> To ordain for these children's sake,
> How they might best lead their life
> Without great dis-ease, care and strife;

> And most for the multitude that was coming
> Of their children after great clerks,
> To teach them then good works;

The first sentence was written in Latin, revealing the author to be a highly educated person rather than a lightly trained noble or non-literate stoneworker. The rest appeared in Old English and was composed into rhyming meter extending 794 lines, which also showed a high degree of literacy. The intended audience for the work seemed to include lords and ladies, with an eye toward providing guidance for their families.

Curiously, Regius focused on a specific concern for those families: they often had many children, but only one child could inherit the noble title and lands of the family. What was to be done with the other children who received no income property? The daughters were not a concern, since they could be married off to good families. However the younger sons posed a serious difficulty. In exploring the lives of the Templars we saw their Order was part of the solution to this problem. Younger sons were prodded into taking vows in religious orders. There they became well educated, but lived a dull life—unless they took their vows with the Templars. Then they lived a chivalrous life in a profusely well-endowed order.

With the fall of the Knights Templar, that option no longer existed. This poem suggested Masonry could be appropriate for younger sons who might previously have been urged to be clergy or Templars.

> And pray we them, for our Lord's sake.
> To our children some work to make,
> That they might get their living thereby,
> Both well and honestly full securely.
> In that time, through good geometry,
> This honest craft of good masonry
> Was ordained and made in this manner,
> Counterfeited of these clerks together;
> At these lord's prayers they counterfeited geometry,

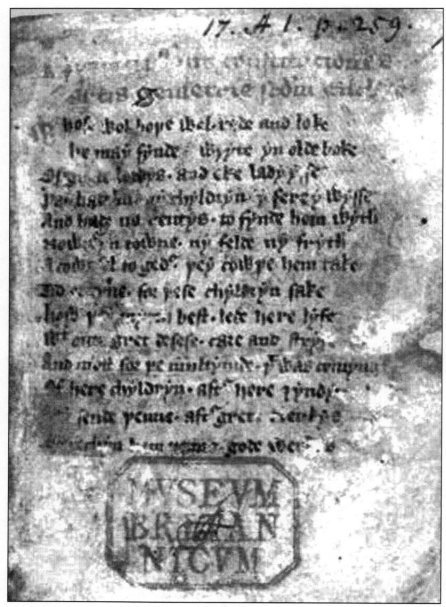

Fig. 28   Regius manuscript

And gave it the name of masonry,
For the most honest craft of all.

Note the observation in Regius that geometry was worked by clerks—which in those days meant clerics—into masonry. There was no known tradition among stonemasons that clerics were the original masons. Within the Templars, however, we saw green-robed clerics arose from among the people who were masons in the Holy Land.

On the face of it, this poem seemed to recommend that younger sons become stonemasons. If that was the case, and if this well-preserved poem had some effect in the world, then history would have recorded a highly unusual trend of gentlemen forsaking their lofty station to work with their hands as stonemasons. Yet no such trend was reported. So the poem either had no effect at all, or its meaning was somewhat deeper.

The answer to this particular puzzle was reflected in the fact that Regius was not recognized as being connected to Freemasonry for many years. It was referred to simply as a poem of moral duties. Oddly enough, that description was one of the things that tied it to Masonry. As every Mason can attest, the tools and practices of the stonemason are used as allegories for life—which is to say that there is another meaning behind the superficial one. That second meaning reflects the Mason's moral duties in life.

Almost everyone knows that a "square" was an L-shaped tool used for making a block of stone or wood truly square or rectangular. Yet in a person's life it meant something was truly good and correct. This led to expressions such as "a square deal," in which the words really do not make any sense outside of Freemasonry. Similarly, the stonemason's "level" insured the stone was being laid properly so that one side was not lower than the other. In life it meant that something was not being tipped or biased unfairly in one direction or another, as in a person being "on the level," or people meeting "on the level" as equals. For many generations, Freemasons actively discussed the use of the square, the level, and similar items as guides for life. Other members of society simply heard interesting expressions and repeated them. Influence in society is not always blunt and direct—sometimes it is quiet and indirect.

The same seemed to be true of Regius. If it was not an actual call for young gentlemen to give up their privileged life and dirty their hands by hewing stones, what was it? Perhaps it was originally intended to call younger sons to make their own way in the world as honest tradesmen and merchants rather than be a drain on the family. Or perhaps it was a straightforward call for young gentlemen to become Freemasons. Given that the poem went on to present the traditional history, articles and points that made up the Old Charges of Freemasonry, this third choice is strongly indicated.

Since all the Old Charges of Freemasonry copied and paraphrased this one document from the 1300s, it is useful to consider the segment of society to which this original appeal was directed. These younger sons of noble families—the same people who once formed the Templars' core membership—now seemed to be prime candidates for Masonry. Since it was normal for people to seek members similar to themselves, it speaks to the composition of the group making this proposal—a well-educated gathering of gentlemen.

Having younger sons of noble families as members of such a group was attractive for other reasons as well. One of the hallmarks of this knightly rebellion was that its members worked together to protect themselves from the arbitrary acts of powerful men, such as those who had crushed the Templars. In this regard younger sons of noble families were not men to be feared. They were not going to inherit the family's estates and power. In fact they were valuable allies. Being brothers in noble families, they were not as easily intimidated by the prospect of having to face an older brother or similar powerful man if that need arose. There was also a further advantage. As younger sons, some of them received a university education in preparation for going into the clergy. That made them similar to the green-robed clerics of the Templars, and similar to the well-educated author of the Regius Manuscript.

Fig. 29 Freemasons meeting "on the level"

Unlike later versions of the Old Charges, the "traditional" history in Regius was quite short. In the equivalent of about eight paragraphs it covered what Anderson's *Constitutions* would cover in forty-eight. The telling of this tale in Regius seemed to be enjoyed by all, so it kept getting longer—being padded with imagined details as time went on.

The seven arts and sciences appeared in Regius and were similar to what was found in Cooke and the other Old Charges. The prayer in Regius was considerably longer than that which appeared in later manuscripts, which would be appropriate for a group that retained influences from a religious order.

The Regius manuscript also referred to "the four crowned ones." These were four martyrs in Rome around 305 AD who refused to forsake their faith, even to the moment of death. The martyrs' situation seemed to resonate with the author.

By some coincidence it also echoed the experience of the captured Templars.

> They were as good masons as on earth shall go,
> Gravers and image-makers they were also.
> For they were workmen of the best,
> The emperor had to them great liking;
> He willed of them an image to make
> That might be worshipped for his sake;
> Such monuments he had in his day,
> To turn the people from Christ's law.
>
> But they were steadfast in Christ's law,
> And to their craft without doubt;
> They loved well God and all his lore,
> And were in his service ever more.
> True men they were in that day,
> And lived well in God's law;
> They thought no monuments for to make,
> For no good that they might take,
> To believe on that monument for their God,
> They would not do so, though he was furious;
> For they would not forsake their true faith,

> And believe on his false law,
> The emperor let take them soon anon,
> And put them in a deep prison;
> The more sorely he punished them in that place,
> The more joy was to them of Christ's grace,
> Then when he saw no other one,
> To death he let them then go;
> By the book he might it show
> In legend of holy ones,
> The names of the four crowned ones.

The "emperor" sought to have them create a false image for all to worship and these men refused, paying the ultimate price. If it was meant to honor fallen Templars, it overlooked the fact that their faith wavered and they confessed to the false image of them. But in the end they were resolute and told the truth, causing many of them to die in flames rather than yield.

The Knights Templar counted among their brothers not only noble-born knights and well-educated clerics, but also serving-men drawn from the rest of society. This was reflected in Regius as well, for it concluded with simple rules of etiquette when in public. Reflecting the different levels of society at that time, it suggested proper deference be shown to a person of higher station. This guidance to working men was brief or missing altogether in the later Old Charges.

> When thou meetest a worthy man,
> Cap and hood thou hold not on;
> In church, in market, or in the gate,
> Do him reverence after his state.
> If thou goest with a worthier man
> Then thyself thou art one,
> Let thy foremost shoulder follow his back,
> For that is nurture without lack;
>
> When he doth speak, hold thee still,
> When he hath done, say for thy will,
> In thy speech that thou be discreet,

And what thou sayest consider thee well;
But deprive thou not him his tale,
Neither at the wine nor at the ale.
Christ then of his high grace,
Save you both wit and space,
Well this book to know and read,
Heaven to have for your reward.
Amen! Amen! so mote it be!
So say we all for charity.

Just as in the Cooke Manuscript, Regius ended with the traditional Masonic closing of "Amen," followed by "So mote it be." This was Freemasonry in its secretive, early days.

Of Knights and Masons

So the mystery of what happened to the fugitive Templars in the 1300s brings us here. The secret ritual of Freemasons contains Medieval French words traced back to the 1300s. The Old Charges of Masonry are actual documents that also date back to that same time. And it is significant to note that no Old Charges or other Masonic document has ever been found from a date earlier than the 1300s.

But stonemasons were present then, so they had an opportunity to create Freemasonry—what of them? In the early 1300s stonemason lodges were in primitive condition. For the most part they were temporary affairs where a castle or cathedral was being raised, or were informal working places in town. Only in the latter part of that century did those lodges begin to get organized and recognized in the leading cities. London's stonemasons gained recognition in 1376 and other cities followed much later. The city of Edinburgh did not recognize its stonemasons until 1475. And no gentlemen were associated with either of these leading lodges in those years—nor even in the 1500s.

Since Freemasonry already existed before most of the signifi-cant Medieval stonemasons lodges were formed, it clearly did not descend from them. And since it existed in the 1300s, its gentlemen, clerics and merchant members were clearly meeting separately from any stonemason activities.

Freemasons and stonemasons existed in parallel during those days. Stonemasons met in dusty lodge rooms filled with blocks of stone in various states of completion, or they met in corners of churches such as St. Giles or Mary's Chapel. Freemasons met in private lodgings or in the wooded countryside, bringing the instruments of their ceremonies with them. As noted earlier, there are no symbols in Masonry related to Medieval stonemasons. All of its symbols are related to antiquity.

On the other hand, the Knights Templar clearly existed before the 1300s. And they were struck down just before the first evidence of Masonry's existence appeared. Yet timing was not the only link between these two societies. There was the white lambskin tied around the waist. Medieval French words explained many Masonic words. A Templar knight with drawn sword stood at the door, followed by a Masonic Tyler at the door wearing the symbol of a drawn sword. The *due guard* used in Masonry tied back to a knight's defensive gesture. Symbols such as the square and compass made further connections.

As it turns out, Templars and Freemasons were also the only two major societies in the world that relied heavily on Solomon's Temple for their foundation. The Knights Templar made their first home at the site of that temple, and named themselves after it. Masonry had its lodge rooms, rituals, practices and symbols largely based on Solomon's Temple. The roles of King Hiram, King Solomon and master mason Hiram Abiff had major parts in those rituals.

The total amount of evidence linking Freemasons with Templars is surprisingly extensive. But when did this relationship begin?

The Templars were at their height during a time when all Christians were Catholic. The Protestant Reformation did not happen until hundreds of years later. If the link between Templars and Masons occurred before 1307, Masons would have been Catholic to the extent they had any religious requirement. That clearly did not happen. The Masonic requirement was that a candidate must believe in God, but beyond that his religion was his own affair. All faiths were accepted, if they had that fundamental belief in God.

This was more in keeping with the state of fugitive Templars after their brothers had suffered and died in the Inquisition. Some brothers abandoned the Catholic faith, while others remained devout. To bridge that gap they had to turn to religious tolerance and make it a requirement among them. This was a perfect fit with what emerged in Masonry. And it points to the connection between Templars and Masons taking place after the knights became fugitives.

The earliest date that could be claimed for former Templars to have become Masons would be the 13th of October 1307, when their Order was struck down and change was forced upon them. On the other hand it may have taken some time for the fugitives to realize their problem was not temporary but instead was permanent. How long might that have been? For these hidden knights to travel to clandestine meetings and carry the tools of their rituals, there was great pressure for them to adopt the cover story of being Masons fairly soon. Whether that happened in days, months or even years after the fugitives began to meet in secret is not known. We can see only that it happened before the Regius manuscript was written later that same century. The words, imagery and Old Charges of Masonry were fully developed and present in this extraordinary document that can still be seen and read today.

So the fugitive Templars called themselves Masons. And they continued to conspire against the forces that had struck them down. But how did their rebellious acts change the world around us?

Sir Thomas

John Wycliffe was an early leader of what became the Protestant Reformation, and paved the way in the 1300s for what came later. His followers believed the accumulation of wealth and power by the Catholic Church had corrupted many of its practices. So they actively called for reform, and became known by the colorful name of Lollards. To the fugitive knights this was a golden opportunity to act against the church inquisitors who had tortured their brothers. So aid was given to these new fugitives from the church. The unsubmissive Lollards soon became known for having an exceptional ability to avoid pursuit by royal and religious authorities. This was attributed at the time to covert aid they received from supporters in the countryside. That covert support was remarkably similar to the practices of the Templar survivors—the rebels being pursued simply disappeared.

Throughout the 1300s and the years that followed, excessive use of force and suppression of dissent by royal and religious leaders drove an endless supply of refugees to seek protection. Many of those fugitives found asylum waiting for them among the rebellious knights now known as Masons. Those fugitives who were deemed worthy were accepted and took on obligations, but

Peasants Revolt 1381 (handwritten)

they only discovered what the Masons were doing one step at a time—that is to say, by degrees.

During those same years another insurgency arose in England that became known as the Peasants' Revolt of 1381. We saw this protest against the abuse of power by state and church proudly claim to have the support of a hidden "Great Society." That support resulted in highly coordinated revolutionary activities all across England. Although the king and church stayed in power this time, the feudal system supporting them began to wither.

Shortly thereafter John Hus succeeded Wycliffe as a major leader of the Protestant revolution. His followers had to defeat five papal crusades against his teachings in the early 1400s. Those isolated displays of resistance then grew to encompass large multitudes of people during the 1500s. Many of those rebels sought protection from the Catholic Church that was fighting to keep its commanding position.

Once the Protestant breakaway was successful in England and other lands, the bloody conflict moved from inquisition cells to the battlefield. Protestant armies and Catholic armies engaged each other in mutual carnage across Europe, and destroyed many towns of "disbelievers." Refugees fled the forces of both sides and needed sanctuary. Freemasonry continued to adapt and flourish during this time.

In Italy, Giovanni di Bicci de' Medici knew how to survive in difficult times. Growing up in Florence during the late 1300s he saw what happened after the destruction of the Templar Order. Those knights who wore the red cross had among their number enough financial geniuses to create the largest banking system in Europe. Their sudden disappearance had left much confusion and a huge void that many rushed to fill.

Fierce competition among small family banks resulted in most of them lasting only a generation or two before lack of skill or bankruptcy forced them to close. Giovanni resolved to be different. He went to work for his cousin who owned a small bank, and quickly rose to become manager of its Rome branch. When the bank split into three parts, the others failed quickly but Giovanni

Fig. 30   Leonardo da Vinci

kept his part afloat and wisely moved it from Rome to his home town of Florence.

It has never been determined if Giovanni was able to recruit men whose grandfathers once wore green Templar robes while administering that brotherhood's vast financial system. But upon his arrival in Florence he began to do business differently. Soon there were branches of Medici Bank all across Europe. Shortly thereafter it became the largest and most trusted bank on the continent.

Thus began the wealth that propelled his Medici family to great prominence in Florence and the surrounding region. That enabled them to lavishly support local artists and give rise to the Renaissance. And few of those creative people was more celebrated than Leonardo da Vinci.

Leonardo was only fourteen when he moved from the outskirts of Florence into the city and became apprenticed to noted artist Verrocchio during 1466. Leonardo's extraordinary artistic ability produced celebrated paintings such as the Mona Lisa and his remarkable The Last Supper. Yet Da Vinci's greatest joy seemed to be his cryptic engineering designs. Carefully recorded in journals that were written backwards, from right to left, they were not always understood but were widely admired as brilliant.

In the generations that followed, one of the Medici family leaders raised his power and prestige to a level higher than most of the others. This was Cosimo I who came to power in 1537. He extended his family's rule over neighboring Siena and the rest of Tuscany, becoming Grand Duke in the process. His prominence was such that four of his successors became popes: Leo X, Clement VII, Pius IV and Leo XI.

Yet Cosimo's gains came at a steep personal cost. His predecessor had been assassinated, and to secure his own position Cosimo had to kill family member Lorenzino de' Medici. In that dangerous environment he felt a strong need to protect himself and avoid prying eyes, so Cosimo built secretive passageways that honeycombed Florence in 1564.

The Vasari Corridor was one such network of passageways. It began at the Palazzo Pitti where the Grand Duke lived, and passed beside Boboli Garden before entering the church of Santa

Felicita. From there it actually crossed the Arno River by running along the Ponte Vecchio or Old Bridge. Once there an elevated passageway extended to the Uffizi or Offices where government administrators were housed. Finally the covert accessway came to the Palazzo Vecchio or Old Palace which was the city's traditional seat of government. These mysterious passageways become a major point of interest in Dan Brown's *Inferno* novel.

In England, Sir Thomas Gresham did not publicly acknowledge being a Templar descendant or a Mason, but his background and actions advanced Masonry and the knightly rebellion to such an extent that it has been a recurring question. He was born into a family of gentlemen who identified themselves as being from the noble line at Gresham manor in Norfolk. Yet he could trace his own heritage back only to John Gresham in 1340 at the nearby town of Aylmerton. This situation would be typical for a younger son or grandson being given a small property but excluded from the primary family title. The father of that John Gresham had his identity obscured for some reason during those post-Templar years.

By the time Sir Thomas was born around 1519, his father and uncle were well established merchants in London. Both men had served as Lord Mayor of London for a period of time, and each had been knighted by King Henry VIII for service to the crown. Using this favorable heritage as a springboard, Thomas went on to exceed both his forbears in the art of trade and financial management, amassing a great fortune in the process. One of the landmarks in his career came in 1565 when he offered to build a central exchange for the City of London, to be used by merchants dealing in foreign trade. All the city had to do was donate the land. The city wisely accepted this offer, and the Royal Exchange was born. Gresham's return for this was a princely £700 per year in rents that he collected from the merchants who opened offices in the Exchange. This widely-celebrated establishment was officially opened by Queen Elizabeth I, who granted use of the royal title.

Beyond all the national recognition, however, there was a more private side to Sir Thomas. It compelled him to write into his will

Fig. 31 Sir Thomas Gresham

that the two crown jewels of his estate, the Exchange and his nearby manor house on Bishopsgate, should be used to create a college for higher education—the first to be built in London. As incredible as it may seem, there were only two universities in England at that time, and they were located in the cities of Oxford and Cambridge. London was unrepresented. After his passing, Gresham College was opened to great acclaim in 1597.

This unique college had several surprising features. It was free of charge to all the citizens of London, with its costs fully covered by Sir Thomas' properties. The subjects being taught were also quite unusual. He funded chairs for professors in geometry, astronomy, physic, law, divinity, rhetoric and music. The last five were the traditional subjects taught in colleges at that time. But neither Cambridge nor Oxford had chairs in geometry or astronomy. Geometry was, however, a central part of Freemasonry. It was seen in the square-and-compass symbol by which Masonry was known around the world. It appeared in the allegories and lessons of Masonry. And we saw the art of geometry given a special place in the Old Charges manuscripts. Sir Thomas also gave it a special place at Gresham College.

His choice of astronomy was a little more subtle. Up to this point, higher education was almost exclusively the domain of the church. As noted earlier, religious clerics were the literate people in Europe, with nobles having a smattering of that art and commons receiving almost none at all. The original purpose of universities was to produce new clerics, and positions as university instructors were almost completely limited to clerics as well. When Henry VIII replaced the Catholic Church with the Church of England in 1534, the new Protestant practitioners simply stepped into the shoes of their Catholic predecessors. As late as the 1700s, graduates of Oxford became ordained ministers before they could teach. The new religious leaders in England continued the long-standing role played by the Catholic Church in determining what was proper education and what was heresy.

In 1543 Nicolaus Copernicus published his controversial finding that the earth revolved around the sun. The Catholic Church denied this as heresy. By 1579 Gresham made his own position clear when he established a professorship to teach astronomy at his college, regardless of the feelings of the church. To put this in perspective, Galileo Galilei publicly declared his support for the findings of Copernicus in 1610 and was put on trial for heresy. He was found guilty, and died under house arrest in Italy.

Thomas Gresham's college would play a major part in breaking the church's control over what could be believed and taught. It was a chance to humble those who had condemned the Templars on false charges of heresy.

Thomas Gresham's College

Sir Robert

One of the remarkable men who came to Gresham College was Sir Robert Moray—a close advisor to several kings, and a Mason active in the Templar rebellion.

Born into a noble family but without a great inheritance, Robert left home in 1633 to join the Scots Guards. He saw this as his chance for adventure, fame and fortune, since the Guards were employed on the continent at that time by Louis XIII of France. That duty allowed Robert to work closely with Cardinal Richelieu—the French cleric and prime minister whose power rivaled that of the king.

Five years later he returned to serve in the Scottish army at Edinburgh. Robert was General of Ordnance when that army invaded England and captured Newcastle-upon-Tyne. Freemasonry came to him there on the 20th of May 1641 when he was initiated by a small delegation from Edinburgh. Robert adopted the five-pointed star as part of his Mason's mark, and employed it often in signing letters from that time forward.

When Cardinal Richelieu died in 1642, it was Robert Moray who carried that news to Charles I, the king who reigned over England, Scotland and Ireland. Those two men's lives became closely entwined from that time forward. Only nine years older than Robert, Charles was the son of King James VI of Scotland. Charles' unfortunate belief in the divine right of kings caused considerable conflict in England, particularly with his weak Parliament. When he declared war on Spain, Parliament attempted to limit his access to funds to prosecute that war. So Charles summarily dismissed the Parliament and began to assess additional taxes without the consent of the governed. Parliament remained disbanded for eleven years.

His relationships in Scotland were not much better. Charles attempted to impose the Church of England's practice of ecumenicalism—where bishops provided leadership—in place of Scottish presbyterianism—where elected members of congregations provided the leadership. That alienated many common people. The Scottish nobility was also angry with Charles for living in London and favoring English nobility for prestigious positions. When the Scottish army invaded England, Charles summoned a new Parliament to approve the Treaty of London, allowing Scots self-determination in religious matters.

But Parliament continued to oppose perceived abuses of power by Charles, so he angrily burst into the House of Commons on the 4th of January 1642 to confront Oliver Cromwell. This launched the English Civil War between the king and his Parliament. Charles transferred his court to Oxford and rallied his army, while Parliament stayed in London and did the same. The devastating war began.

Many Scots saw in England's troubles a chance to side with the king and win additional grants from their distant lord. Others felt a common cause with the Parliamentarians. It was during these tumultuous days that Robert Moray and Charles grew closer. The king saw real value in this Scot who knew his way around the French court, and asked for Robert's help. He honored Robert by conferring a knighthood upon him in January of 1643, and sent him to France as the crown's emissary. These things would prove to be valuable to Sir Robert in advancing the quiet rebellion to which he belonged.

Robert found himself in serious difficulty when King Louis XIII of France died four months later. That left the Scottish knight without influence in the new French court. Still only thirty-four years of age, Robert was resilient enough to start again by accepting a commission as Colonel of the Scots Guard in the service of the French king. Campaigning in Germany, he was captured and held in Bavaria for ransom, but gained his release in 1645.

While recovering from this ordeal, Sir Robert learned that the army of Charles I had been destroyed by the forces of Parliament under Cromwell. Rather than surrender to English Parliament forces, Charles gave himself up to the Scottish army near Nottingham. Robert rushed back from France to participate in the difficult negotiations to win Charles' release. There he walked beside the king in the woods made famous by a man named Robin Hood, and counseled the king to escape. Upon hearing that the plan called for him to dress like a woman, Charles indignantly refused and remained in captivity.

Eventually peace came, but it was not long-lasting. By early 1648 Charles rallied enough support to start the Civil War again. Exasperated, Oliver Cromwell and other Parliamentary leaders put Charles on trial at Westminster for high treason. He was publicly executed on the 30th of January 1649.

Sir Robert had hoped to win more concessions for Scots and the common people, like the ones Charles gave in 1641, but that avenue was now cut off. So he hastened to France where the late king's son, also named Charles, lived in exile. There Robert and other Scots persuaded the young Prince of Wales to return to Scone, the ancestral home of Scottish kings located north of Edinburgh. In that auspicious place the royal heir was crowned King Charles II of Scotland on the 1st of January 1651. The new king was so grateful to Sir Robert that he seemed unable to refuse him anything thereafter.

To add the English crown to his Scottish one, Charles set off at the head of a military force—made up chiefly of Scots—to confront the Parliamentary army. This major battle happened at Worcester in Western England during September of 1651, but did not turn out well for the young monarch. He was compelled to retreat from the field, and had to take up residence in France once again.

Sir Robert stayed in Scotland this time, accepting the position of Lord Justice Clerk, one of the highest judicial seats in the land. He was also named a Privy Councillor, or personal advisor to the king. After Robert joined an unsuccessful Scottish uprising in 1653 against English rule, he judiciously spent several years in continental Europe with Charles II.

The death of Oliver Cromwell five years later left Parliamentarians in England divided and unable to rule. As a last resort, they agreed to the return of young Charles, and to his being crowned king of England and Ireland. The Scottish monarch returned to England and began his reign there on the 29th of May 1660. His formal coronation came later at Westminster Abbey, not far from where his father had been executed eleven years earlier.

And a new day began for Sir Robert and his fellow conspirators.

Royal Society

Only a few months after Sir Robert Moray helped Charles take his place as king of England, he found himself at an historic meeting in Gresham College. He was well aware that the men who gathered there on the 28th of November 1660 were involved in a plot to overthrow the control held by church and state over what could be believed and declared in the realm.

Those whispers of conspiracy began when the Templars were accused of heresy, tortured and disbanded. They grew into acts of disobedience and the sheltering of fugitives from king and church, then into the sheltering of revolutionaries. Now their course shifted into assertive action as Sir Robert and other members of the secretive group known as the Invisible College came together to storm the barricades of power. This was not the only action being taken by the quiet Templar rebellion, but it was one of the most important.

The cautionary tale of Galileo was still fresh in the minds of the men who gathered in this particular gathering. That gentleman had died under house arrest only eighteen years earlier for the heresy of declaring that the earth revolved around the sun. Sir Robert's co-conspirators at Gresham College had made many sci-

Galileo

entific discoveries about the world, and did so without the permission of the church. That meant they risked denunciation—and the punishment Galileo received—each time they dared put some part of their findings forward to the public. Their animated discussion that night in 1660 turned to the need for the king's stamp of approval on their inquiries—an official imprimatur—so they could publish without fear of arrest or charges of heresy. If they could break free of the church's tight grip, they hoped for a revolution that could change the life of every person, high and low.

Church leaders feared that such dabbling might lead to things as outrageous as Darwin's theory of evolution—which might directly contradict the Bible. Their fears were well founded.

One of the other men around whom these plotters gathered was Christopher Wren, the professor of astronomy at Gresham College. It was after his lecture at the college that this fateful meeting was held. Just like Moray, Wren was a Freemason and shared the long heritage of trying to break free from the church's control.

Yet Sir Robert could see this event at Gresham was not a wholly Masonic meeting. Even though a number of practices from Masonry were incorporated into their proceedings, the group did not meet with full Masonic ceremony and observances. This indicated that some of the participants were not Masons but simply shared the same values as those who were members.

They certainly did not look like typical revolutionaries—who might have worked by candlelight in musty cellars while writing emotional manifestos. Instead this cabal of twelve gentlemen met in well-appointed rooms for serious planning. Even so, they met in complete secrecy due to the risks attached to what they were doing. As a result they became known as the Invisible College.

John Wallis, another active member of the group, described their meetings this way.

> About the year 1645...we did by agreement, divers of us, meet weekly in London on a certain day.... Our business was (precluding matters of Theology and State Affairs) to discourse and consider of Philosophical Enquiries, and such as related there-unto; as Physick, Anatomy, Geometry, Astronomy, Navigation,

Fig. 32   Galileo

Staticks, Magneticks, Chymicks, Mechanicks, and Natural Experiments....

About the year 1648/1649, some of our company being removed to Oxford (first Dr. Wilkins, then I, and soon after Dr. Goddard) our company divided. Those in London continued to meet there as before (and we with them, when we had occasion to be there)....[27]

Wallis noted a strange practice in the gatherings in addition to secrecy. The proceedings banned "matters of Theology and State Affairs." In other words, religion and politics were off limits.

As every Freemason knows, a firm prohibition exists against the discussion of religion or politics in any Masonic meeting. This reflected their order's birth in the events that shattered the Templars.

This rule shared by the Invisible College and Masonry produced surprising results. Consider a fourth member of the "college," John Wilkins, who graduated from Oxford and became a professor. In 1641 he anonymously published the first book in English on cryptography codes. Anonymous publication was a way to get around the risk of publishing new material that could draw accusations of heresy or treason. His work led to the invention of the telegraph. Dr. Wilkins then married the sister of Oliver Cromwell. Cromwell was at that time Lord Protector of England, and arranged for Wilkins to become Master of the prestigious Trinity College at Cambridge University. In other words, he was deeply involved on the Parliamentarian side in the English Civil War.

Sir Robert Moray, on the other hand had been a personal advisor to Charles I and held an even closer role with his son, Charles II. Few would have been identified as closer to the royal side in this civil war. So how could John Wilkins, brother-in-law to Oliver Cromwell, be involved in the Invisible College with Sir Robert? It should be remembered that Cromwell presided over the execution of young Charles' father. Charles II returned the favor by having Cromwell's body dug up and decapitated posthumously. If the subject of politics had ever come up, Wilkins and Sir Robert would surely have been at each other's throat. But the Masonic

Oxford

rule was applied, and neither man spoke of religion or politics in those meetings. In the absence of that divisive discussion, they developed a deep respect for each other's abilities and contributions. In this critical meeting held at Gresham College, Sir Robert was chosen as president of the group, and Dr. Wilkins was named its secretary.

It is also notable that Oxford was considered the most suitable place for members of the Invisible College to live and work outside of London. Many Masons gathered there, including Elias Ashmole who founded the famous Ashmolean museum on its campus. Among other unexplored questions involving Oxford was the matter of the Knights Templar presence in that city.

When first Templar Grand Master came to England in 1128, Oxford was the only university in Britain. It reasonably drew the attention of the literate administrative brothers who accompanied him. Years later, when the Sandford estate near Oxford was donated to the Templars, it was quickly elevated to serve as an important Templar center. This estate was bounded by Temple Road, Marsh Road, and Oxford Road, only one-and-a-half miles from Magdalen College on the Oxford University campus. This was a distance that could be walked in thirty minutes. Being a prominent estate, it was not possible to conceal this Oxford land when disaster struck in 1307. So the displaced Templars were forced to abandon it and find other accommodations in the area. It would be intriguing to explore someday into what happened at Oxford with the Templars, the Invisible College and Masonry.

Sir Robert Moray was chosen to lead this clandestine group in part because he came to the Invisible College fresh from helping to install the new king of England. He had unparalleled access to the crown, and was prepared to use it. On that auspicious night at Gresham the plotters formalized their plan, and Sir Robert gave them his commitment to carry it forward to the king. By that simple act, the Royal Society came into being.

Sir Robert kept his word and met with Charles II, obtaining for his compatriots a formal Charter of Incorporation on the 15th of July 1662.

Royal Society

This Royal Society quickly became a Who's Who of famous people, not just from England but many other countries as well. Nor was it simply a social club. Its members began to produce a stream of discoveries that extensively expanded our knowledge of the arts and sciences. Sir Isaac Newton made contributions on gravity and physics, Christopher Wren improved architecture. Robert Hooke created the term "cell" to describe the basic unit of life. Benjamin Franklin, another well-known Mason, made contributions on electricity.

And yes, Charles Darwin was a member, then received the society's Royal Medal for his work on evolution.

The Templar rebellion against the power of kings and church had succeeded against one of those two citadels. The Vatican's worst fears had finally been realized. With the formation of the Royal Society, the church lost its power to cry "heresy" and control what was discovered, taught and believed.

This was a victory those early, fugitive Templars—stung by the Inquisition—had prayed for but could not confidently have expected. Yet it had happened.

And another change was coming that would break the power of kings.

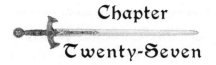
Sir Christopher

When a devastating fire leveled most of London in 1666 the king called upon Sir Christopher Wren, known to him from the Royal Society, to rebuild the city. That monumental task would take the rest of Sir Christopher's life and included his magnificent work on St. Paul's Cathedral. Yet his greatest contributions were the ones he made out of public view, for he served the cause of the Templar resistance well. He made certain that the Royal Society succeeded by serving as its president during 1680-1682, even though he was loathe to hold a public office other than his architectural duties. Through all these things he stayed active in English society at a level just below the king while a series of events took place which were critical to his secretive society.

Charles II unwittingly launched this series of events in 1685 when he passed away without producing a legitimate heir. The twelve illegitimate children he brought into the world were regrettably unable to inherit. So his crown passed to his brother James. That act elevated his brother to be James II of England and Ireland, as well as James VII of Scotland. Normally this would not have caused a problem, but James had converted to the Roman Catholic faith. And he now wore the crown of the kingdom that

Henry VIII had split away from Catholicism in 1534 to create the powerful Church of England. This Anglican Church was the one to which most of his subjects now belonged.

Undaunted, James began laboring to roll back the Protestant tide by appointing Catholics to senior positions—an act that did not sit well with the general populace. These stark religious differences were aggravated by James' belief in the absolute power of kings. This was the same belief that had gotten his father, Charles I, beheaded in public. It therefore came as no surprise to Sir Christopher and his contemporaries when James had to weather two revolts against the crown during the first year of his reign. These he quickly put down, but outspoken opposition by Parliament continued until he felt compelled to disband that body. It did not meet again during his reign.

Miraculously, in spite of these difficulties it seemed that James might yet weather the problems that beset him. This was due to both of his daughters being Protestants. One of them, Mary, was also married to the Protestant William of Orange, who ruled the Dutch Republic. Although manifestly unhappy, the not-so-loyal opposition seemed resigned to tolerating James' reign and waiting for the happy day when one of his children would ascend the throne. Then in 1688 James had a son by his Catholic wife, and everything changed. The existence of a Catholic heir caused uprisings to break out across the land with greater force than ever before. This was the moment for which Wren's secret society had been waiting.

Much like the Peasants' Revolt three hundred years earlier, well-coordinated support across the land brought this groundswell to a crest of full rebellion. It became known as the *Glorious Revolution of 1688.* Those massive protests grew into military campaigns when James' daughter Mary and her husband William of Orange arrived in England from the Netherlands at the head of an army. Their force was soon joined by many English leaders and troops, allowing the revolution to press forward strongly.

In less than gallant manner, James decided not to fight and instead threw the Great Seal of the Realm into the River Thames. Then he promptly fled to France. A Parliament was assembled to deal with the situation, and it quickly decided that James' actions amounted to abdication. As a result, the crown was offered to his daughter Mary and her husband William, to rule jointly—but only under specific written conditions.

This was an extremely rare occurrence—to have members of the public confront a monarch with conditions before granting a crown. It reflected deep resentment in Britain against the excesses of power exercised by previous kings and queens. One of the clearest examples of excessive use of power was the harsh treatment inflicted on the Knights Templar. It left a striking and vivid picture in people's minds of king and church wrongfully taking people's life, liberty and property—with no recourse but what the king or church might give. Inquisitions, executions and the recent civil war had kept those fears fresh.

The list of conditions limiting William and Mary were made clear to them, and the new royal couple approved those terms. Parliament then formally ratified this English Bill of Rights. The bill contained a few provisions related directly to the English situation—such as rules governing the succession of monarchs—but many of its other provisions were echoed later in the United States Bill of Rights.

The charter of the Royal Society had embodied the strong desire to remove arbitrary rule by the church. The English Bill of Rights now removed the arbitrary power of the king. And that was not its only similarity with the Royal Society charter.

This newly-adopted certificate of rights was a strange creation. It represented neither a sole victory for the Parliamentary forces, nor a sole victory for Royalist partisans. The recent revolution had led to confrontations over whether to continue the powerful monarchy or dismiss the king as the previous Civil War had done. Now, for some reason, another force had emerged. It reached people on both sides of this divisive issue, and brought them together to meet in the middle. There they agreed on the compromise that was artfully penned. It protected people from exercise of arbitrary power, rather than following the extremes of the previous Civil War.

Similar to what happened in the Invisible College and Royal Society, it would be wrong to think a remarkable outcome like this was driven only by an invisible secret society such as that created

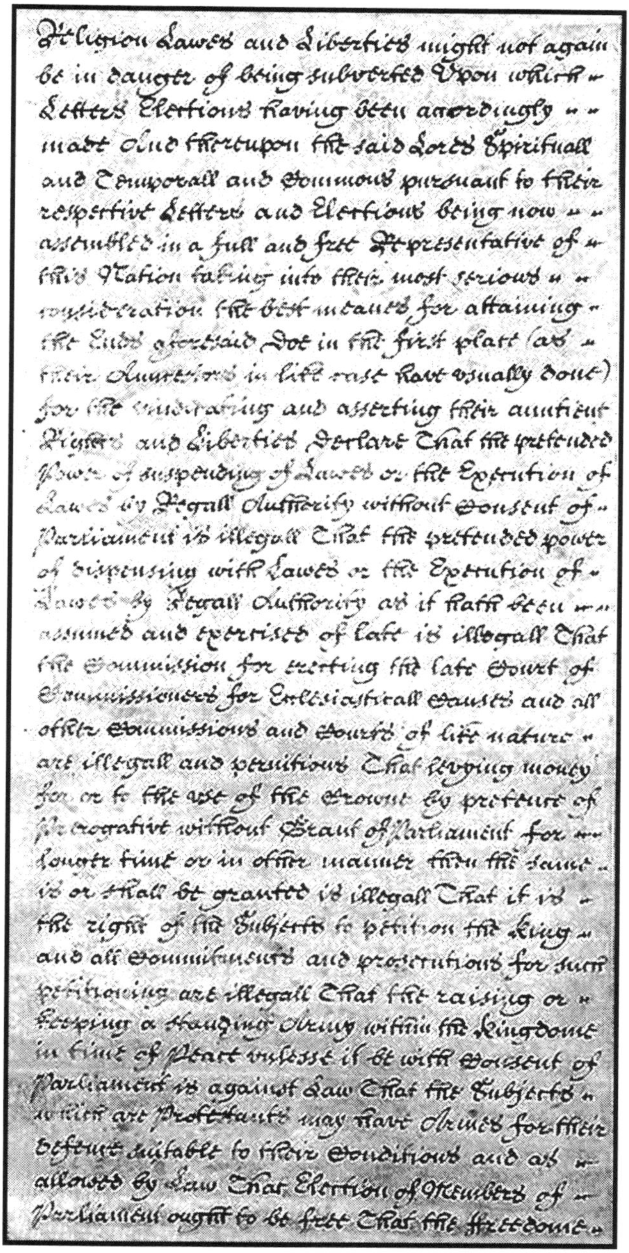

Religion Lawes and Liberties might not again be in danger of being subverted Upon which Letters Elections having been accordingly made and thereupon the said Lords Spirituall and Temporall and Commons pursuant to their respective Letters and Elections being now assembled in a full and free Representative of this Nation taking into their most serious consideration the best meanes for attaining the Ends aforesaid Doe in the first place (as their Auncestors in like case have usually done) for the vindicating and asserting their auntient Rights and Liberties Declare That the pretended Power of suspending of Lawes or the Execution of Lawes by Regall Authority without Consent of Parliament is illegall That the pretended power of dispensing with Lawes or the Execution of Lawes by Regall Authority as it hath beene assumed and exercised of late is illegall That the Commission for erecting the late Court of Commissioners for Ecclesiasticall Causes and all other Commissions and Courts of like nature are illegall and pernicious That levying money for or to the use of the Crowne by pretence of Prerogative without Grant of Parliament for longer time or in other manner then the same is or shall be granted is illegall That it is the right of the Subjects to petition the King and all Commitments and Prosecutions for such petitioning are illegall That the raising or keeping a standing Army within the Kingdome in time of Peace unlesse it be with Consent of Parliament is against Law That the Subjects which are Protestants may have Armes for their defence suitable to their Conditions and as allowed by Law That Election of Members of Parliament ought to be free That the freedome

Fig.33   English Bill of Rights

by the fugitive Templars which became known as Masonry. Clear-ly there were other large and powerful forces at work. The nose-to-nose confrontation of Catholics and Protestants could not be denied. Nor could the Parliamentarian versus Royalist confronta-tions be underestimated. Those forces were strong enough to lead to bloodshed, as they had before. Yet despite those volatile forces being present, no explosion occurred this time.

Instead events followed a process like the one that formed the Royal Society. There, in what could have been an extremely tense situation, the brother-in-law of Lord Protector Oliver Cromwell faced the Privy Councillor to the King—and took each other by the hand instead of by the throat. What John Wilkins and Sir Rob-ert Moray had done in private, now lords and commons did in public. The force of this public agreement was such that the king and queen were required to accept these limits on their power. It was a new moment, and a new day.

This knightly rebellion had maintained its secret existence for so many years, waiting for the abusive physical power of king and church to be broken.

Had it finally happened? Was this Bill of Rights enough of a re-straint on the king? And if it was, then would this restraint last, or would it soon be overthrown in a return to the bloody excesses of the past? Those living in the shadows had to wait a little longer to see what would happen. These limits had to pass the test of time and successive coronations.

As fortune would have it, the next several reigns passed somewhat quickly.

Queen Mary died five years after she was crowned, leaving William to rule alone. He passed away in 1702, conferring the throne upon Mary's sister, Anne. Although Queen Anne was the second daughter of James II, she did not go back to his policies. The Bill of Rights remained in full force and effect. After a reign of twelve years, she left the crown to distant relative George I in 1714. Having passed through the reigns of all these men and women, it seemed clear the protections were going to last. There was still a king, so more needed to be done. But this was a mile-stone and a good victory.

It seemed to be enough that there was no more need for secrecy. The conspirators began to cautiously emerge.

Members of several Masonic lodges discussed coming fully into public view. If this was done, however, it would be a step that could not be undone later. So the decision was not taken lightly. Sir Christopher joined other brothers and lodges in waiting and watching the actions of his more outspoken brethren. When the day finally came, only four lodges were bold enough to step forward.

John Desaguliers

$\mathcal{T}$ he knightly society known as Masonry was described by Robert Plot in his 1686 book *Natural History of Staffordshire*, a county in the English Midlands. This preview came just before the secretive society fully emerged into public view.

> ...the *Customs* relating to the *County*, whereof they have one, of admitting Men into the *Society of Freemasons*, that in the *moorelands* of this *County* seems to be of greater request, than any where else, though I find the *Custom* spread more or less all over the *Nation*; for here I found persons of the most eminent quality, that did not disdain to be of this *Fellowship*.
>
> Into which *Society* when any are admitted, they call a *meeting* (or *Lodg* as they term it in some places) which must consist at lest of 5 or 6 of the *Ancients* of the *Order*, whom the *candidates* present with *gloves*, and so likewise to their *wives*, and entertain with a *collation* according to the Custom of the place. This ended, they proceed to the *admission* of them, which chiefly consists in the communication of certain *secret*

signes, whereby they are known to one another all over the *Nation*, by which means they have maintenance whither ever they travel: for if any man appear though altogether unknown that can shew any of these *signes* to a *Fellow* of the *Society*, whom they otherwise call an *accepted mason*, he is obliged presently to come to him, from what company or place soever he be in, nay tho' from the top of a *Steeple*, (what hazard or inconvenience soever he run) to know his pleasure, and assist him: *viz.* if he want *work* he is bound to find him some; or if he cannot do that, to give him *mony*, or otherwise support him till *work* can be had.[28]

These customs are still very much alive in Masonic practices. Yorkshire and Northern England had a number of highly active lodges in these years. The Old Lodge at York recorded that the position of President or Master in this Lodge was held by a series of gentlemen between 1705 and 1713, including knights, baronets, and the lord mayor of York.

But the first step toward full emergence of this secretive society came in London.

One Mason seemed to have a more far-reaching involvement than any other when he strode into the Apple-Tree Tavern to negotiate the creation of the Grand Lodge in 1717. His name was John Desaguliers, one of the early Grand Masters.

John had graduated from the University of Oxford in 1709, then landed a choice position as assistant to Sir Isaac Newton. The venerable Sir Isaac sponsored him for membership in the prestigious Royal Society, then introduced him to many members of London's higher social circles.

It was around this time that John became active as a Mason in the lodge that met at the Rummer and Grapes Tavern in Channel Row, Westminster. And when four of the old lodges got together to discuss forming a Grand Lodge, the Rummer and Grapes was well represented. Other instigators came from the lodge that met at the Goose and Gridiron Ale-house in St. Paul's Churchyard, the lodge at the Crown Ale-house near Drury Lane, and the one at the

Apple-Tree Tavern in Covent Garden. Those events were described in the *New Book of Constitutions* written in 1738.

> They and some old Brothers met at the said *Apple-Tree*, and having put into the Chair the *oldest Master* Mason (now the *Master* of a *Lodge*) they constituted themselves a GRAND LODGE pro Tempore in *Due Form*, and forthwith revived the Quarterly *Communication* of the *Officers* of Lodges (call'd the Grand Lodge) resolv'd to hold the *Annual* ASSEMBLY *and Feast*, and then to chuse a GRAND MASTER from among themselves, till they should have the Honour of a *Noble Brother* at their Head.

Accordingly

> On St. *John Baptist's* Day, in the 3d Year of King George I. *A.D.* 1717. the ASSEMBLY and *Feast* of the *Free and accepted Masons* was held at the foresaid *Goose and Gridiron* Ale-house.
>
> Before Dinner, the *oldest Master* Mason (now the *Master of a Lodge*) in the Chair, proposed a list of proper Candidates; and the Brethren by a Majority of Hands elected
>
> Mr. ANTONY SAYER Gentleman, *Grand Master* of *Masons*, [and Capt. *Joseph Elliot*, Mr. *Jacob Lamball, Carpenter—Grand Wardens*] who being forthwith invested with the Badges of Office and Power by the said *oldest Master*, and install'd, was duly congratulated by the Assembly who pay'd him the *Homage*.

With that grand event, Freemasonry emerged from secrecy and became a visible member of society. Two years later John Desaguliers was chosen by his peers to serve as Grand Master. When he accepted this position the Grand Lodge seemed to take a significant leap forward. Aristocratic members of the London community showed more interest and began to join, elevating the public perception of Masonry. He also served as Master of various "Occasional Lodges" where members of nobility were made Masons.

Fig. 34   Goose and Gridiron Ale-house

On one such occasion he raised as a Mason the Prince of Wales, who later became King George II.

In addition to exchanging gloves with nobility, John also had a strong commitment to his family. He married Joanna Pudsey and she gave him seven children. Unfortunately the happiness she brought him was tempered by the tragic loss of many of their children. Only two of them survived infancy and lived to adulthood. When John's own time came in February of 1744, the Royal Society noted with proper respect that he was buried at the Savoy Chapel on the Strand in Westminster.

By coming into the open and creating a Grand Lodge, John Desaguliers and his brethren established an example that was soon followed by all Masons. The Templar rebellion still had the same roots and continued to grow, but now it was partially out in the daylight.

Benjamin Franklin

Irish Masons continued their secretive ways when they formed their own Grand Lodge in Dublin. They made no record of that body's founding and allowed it to became known to Irish society only through this notice in the *Dublin Weekly Journal* on the 25th of June 1725.

> Thursday last, being St. John's Day, Patron of the Most Antient, and Rt. Worshipful Society of Freemasons; they met about Eleven o' the Clock, at the Yellow Lion in Warbroughs-street, where there appear'd above a 100 Gentlemen. After some time spent, in putting on their Aprons, White Gloves, and other parts of the *Distinguishing* Dress of that Worshipful Order, they proceeded over Essex-Bridge to the Strand, and from thence to the King's Inns….

In that same year the Old Lodge of York launched the "Grand Lodge of All England at York." This declaration came as something of a shock to the Grand Lodge in London. The York proclamation was quickly followed by that of another Grand Lodge in the county of Chester. To head off this growing wave of Northern defections, the Grand Lodge in London adeptly persuaded the brothers in Chester to accept the title of Provincial Grand Lodge and to operate under London's guidance. This curious arrangement of establishing "Provincial" Grand Lodges was then repeated in numerous other counties.

Provincial Grand Lodges also cropped up among the colonies of North America. Masons had met in ad-hoc American lodges ever since they first arrived in wooden sailing boats and started to hew farms, towns and cities out of the wilderness. The Grand Lodge of England acknowledged their growing status by granting a patent to Daniel Coxe in 1730 to serve as Provincial Grand Master for New York, New Jersey and Pennsylvania. However there was no indication that he ever exercised that authority.

In Pennsylvania, local lodges elected William Allen to be their Provincial Grand Master in 1732, but not much happened until Benjamin Franklin was chosen to serve as the colony's Provincial Grand Master in 1734.

Ben Franklin was only twelve years old in 1718 when he started down the path that brought him to international acclaim and Masonry. Serving as an apprentice printer to his older brother in Boston was educational, but he yearned to make his own way in the world. So five years later he moved to Philadelphia, and then set sail for London. There he found employment as typesetter for a printing house located in the decommissioned church of St. Bartholomew the Great, more popularly known as St. Bart's. The ragtag commercial rooms built onto the side of the church can still be seen today. His daily work at St. Bart's was only a few blocks north of St. Paul's Cathedral, in whose courtyard resided one of the four Masonic lodges that brought Freemasonry into the open seven years earlier. Ben lived in the epicenter of Masonry at that time, but being only nineteen he did not yet enter this society.

The whirlwind of his life began in earnest when he returned to America, settled in Philadelphia and became a respected printer in his own right. Ben gained great acclaim by publishing the *Pennsylvania Gazette,* which rapidly became one of the leading news-

Fig. 35   Benjamin Franklin

papers of that day. It also caused him to emerge as a social leader in the city.

When he turned twenty-five Ben took a significant step by entering St. John's Lodge and becoming a Mason. Three years later his energy and popularity had elevated him to the role of Provincial Grand Master for Pennsylvania. That same year he re-printed *The Constitutions of the Free-Masons*, originally published in England, to share Masonry with other men he was meeting in colonial America. Since these colonies would not issue their famous Declaration of Independence—on the way to becoming the United States of America—until forty-two years later, it would be fair to say that Ben helped Freemasonry become rooted in the New World.

Around that same time, far to the south on the rugged American coastline, a Mason named James Oglethorpe established the colony of Georgia. James had grown up near London under the guidance of parents well-connected in society. He left Oxford University to pursue other interests and eventually wound up in Parliament. Once there, he strongly advocated the traditional Masonic position of opposing debtors' prisons. Toward that end he proposed to re-settle debtors to a new colony to be named Georgia, where each would receive land and work to support themselves. His proposal was approved and he set out at the head of the first group of colonists to create a settlement near the current location of Savannah in Georgia.

James opened the first Masonic lodge in that colony during 1734 and it became known as Solomon's Lodge Number 1. He also served as the group's first Worshipful Master. In 1735 the Grand Lodge of England appointed a member of that lodge, Roger Lacey, to serve as Provincial Grand Master for Georgia.

Shortly thereafter the colony of New York finally got its own Provincial Grand Master when Captain Richard Riggs accepted his appointment there.

Scotland then followed suit, having waited until 1736 to create a Grand Lodge of its own. There was a longstanding tradition of Masonry in Scotland. But that country had an even longer tradition of proud independence. When those two forces finally reached a good balance, the Masonic lodges yielded their independence and came together to form the Grand Lodge of Scotland. The assembled brethren chose William St. Clair as their first Grand Master, and thereby began a new tradition rooted in the old.

Only two years after Scottish Masons took that step, this long-lived society of fugitive Templars faced a serious threat. It came about as the unintended result of a Scottish knight's efforts in France.

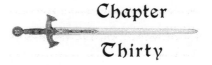

Chevalier Ramsay

Andrew Ramsay hardly seemed like the kind of person to trigger opposing waves of euphoria and dread over connections between the Templars and Masons. The son of a common baker in Ayr, Scotland, thirty miles southwest of Glasgow, he was good enough with books to gain admission to the University of Edinburgh in 1700 at the tender age of fourteen. Three years later he put his youth and education to good use by tutoring a succession of prominent men's sons. This occupation brought him to France where his tutoring brought him in touch with highly-placed members of the royal court.

Among those French leaders was the Archbishop of Cambrai who converted Andrew to Roman Catholicism. This was a remarkable accomplishment, since Andrew was—and continued to be—a practitioner of the *Quietism* cult that had been condemned by several popes. His circle of friends in Paris grew to include Philippe d'Orleans who served as Regent of France and ruled that country on behalf of five-year-old Louis XV. It was from the Regent's hands that Andrew received the Order of St. Lazarus, which conferred upon him the title of *Chevalier*, or French knight. As Chevalier Ramsay he wrote several books and received the distinction of an honorary doctorate at Oxford. At that same time, in March of 1730, he was initiated as a Freemason at the Horn Lodge of London.

Andrew's involvement with Masonry deepened when he returned to France, and by 1737 he was the Grand Orator in Paris. In that capacity he produced the work that cast him into the pages of history. From his pen flowed the "Discourse pronounced at the reception of Freemasons." This soon gained both fame and notoriety as *Chevalier Ramsay's Oration*. It traced the roots of Masonry not to stonemasons as others had done, but to the knights of the Crusades.

> At the time of the Crusades in Palestine many princes, lords, and citizens associated themselves, and vowed to restore the Temple of the Christians in the Holy Land, to employ themselves in bringing back their architecture to its first institution. They agreed upon several ancient signs and symbolic words drawn from the well of religion in order to recognize themselves amongst the heathen and Saracens. These signs and words were only communicated to those who promised solemnly, and even sometimes at the foot of the altar, never to reveal them.... Sometime afterwards our Order formed an intimate union with the Knights of St. John of Jerusalem.[29]

Although he did not directly name the Templars in his oration, the Knights of St. John—otherwise known as the Hospitallers—were united with only one other order, and that was the Knights Templar. Andrew did not get the time of connection between Templars and Masons quite right—attributing it to when the knights were at the height of their power rather than when they were fugitives—but the direction and connection were correct. And his findings resonated with many people. Word of Andrew's revelation generated a surge of interest in this knightly heritage of Masonry. Ripples of excitement crossed the borders of France into neighboring lands, and spread across the Channel into Great Britain.

Yet before that positive wave swept north, a bitterly negative wave swept south. This came from Andrew's assumption that the air of knighthood in his oration would be appreciated in the court of Louis XV. Accordingly he sent a copy of his speech to Cardinal Fleury, the king's prime minister, in March of 1737. The sharp rejection of Ramsay's oration by Cardinal Fleury revealed that this commentary on the connection between Templars and Masons had touched a raw nerve.

It was no secret that the Templars had been brutally tortured and burned at the stake by representatives of the Vatican. So the possibility that brothers-in-arms or family members of fallen knights might take revenge against the Catholic Church was a natural concern to Cardinal officers of the Vatican for many years.

That fear seemed to still be in the air, for when Andrew issued his oration linking Templars and Masons it was like a match thrown onto fuel-soaked kindling. There was an immediate eruption. Within eleven days, Cardinal Fleury issued an interdict banning all Masonic meetings in France. He and other Cardinals then involved the pope in Rome.

Pope Clement XII responded by publishing his papal bull *In eminenti* condemning Freemasonry on the 28th of April 1738.

Clearly the church or any other group was entitled to defend itself when attacked. Over the centuries there was no question that kings such as Philip IV of France and leaders of other religions had attacked the church. Responding to those actions in the form of an official papal bull was quite reasonable.

What made *In eminenti* so unusual was that the now-public organization identified as Masonry was not known to have done anything to attack or harm the Catholic Church during the twenty-one years since it came into public view. Nor did the pope's document give any specific cause for the pope's action. He attributed his motivation only to having heard "common gossip" and "rumors" about Freemasonry. That was deemed enough to publish a public condemnation and declare excommunication. If this sounds too ridiculous to be believed, feel free to visit the Vatican website and read the full text.

Clement said he had the "greatest suspicion" that Masons were doing something wrong, and that they must be "depraved and perverted." He succinctly summed up the charges this way, "For if they were not doing evil they would not have so great a hatred of the light." In other words, if he did not know what they were doing, they must be doing evil. What was the appropriate punishment for keeping secrets? Freemasons were "condemned and prohibited," and anyone involved with them or helping them in any way was to suffer the "pain of excommunication."

Perhaps even more curious than this strange argument was that the Vatican took any action at all. By the time this papal order was written, the highest imaginable number of visible Masonic lodges worldwide would have been on the order of 600. That would have meant a total membership of 15,000 to 30,000 at the most. This was about the same population as one good-sized town. In a world of roughly 750 million people at that time, how could such a small number of individuals possibly be worth the pope's attention, let alone a formal letter attempting to charge them with a vague offence?

This over-reaction to Masonry was as if the Vatican saw a feared old foe re-emerging on the battlefield. *In eminenti* even borrowed some of the language and actions used against the Templars by the earlier pope. In this new condemnation Clement XII ordered "inquisitors for heresy" into the fray against Freemasons. Then without waiting for inquisitors to take to the field and find any wrong-doing by Masons, the pope proceeded directly to punishment, instructing his inquisitors that they "are to pursue and punish them with condign penalties as being most suspect of heresy."

How much did their questionable actions against the Templars still cause burning concern within the Vatican? Consider what happened when court records from Jacques de Molay's first trial were recently found.

Chi non
Parchment
1308

Proceeding Against the Templars

A rare document discovered in the Vatican Secret Archives revived long-simmering concerns over the controversial actions
taken against the Templars. This was the *Chinon Parchment.* Written in France during 1308, it was "misplaced" by the Vatican for
700 years, then suddenly rediscovered in its Archives during 2001.
People affiliated with the Vatican promptly declared that this
document exonerated the church for its actions against the Templars. They also asserted *Chinon* cleared the record of this knightly
order by finding those men innocent of the charges of heresy
against them.

But those claims were not true. This became evident when
those records were published by the Vatican in 2007 as *Processus
Contra Templarios,* which means "proceeding against the Templars."

When King Philip arrested hundreds of Templars in France on
the 13th of October 1307, Pope Clement V insisted on his right to
try his own people. This was a long-standing tradition designed to
keep the church independent of rule or punishment by kings.
Having demanded his right, Clement sent three cardinals to the

city of Chinon in Western France for the first great trial of Jacques de Molay and the other leaders of the Knights Templar.

The proceedings from that trial were duly recorded by scribes on what became the *Chinon Parchment*. It showed de Molay and the other men were brought from prison to the trial chamber where they repeated their earlier confession of acts which could be considered heresy, and repented. In return they were absolved and reconciled with the Church. This amounted to a "plea bargain" in which they pled guilty to less than all of the charges against them. Other Templars had already signed similar confessions and gained their freedom, so the leaders of the Templars no doubt expected the same treatment. Yet their freedom did not come.

It was possible that this trial and the parchment at Chinon may have been valiant attempts by the pope to save his people and, if that was true, be a highly commendable act. Yet the pope's actions from that moment forward lend themselves to no such gentle interpretation.

The following year, before any of the Templars in Great Britain had been called as witnesses to support or rebut the accusations against them, the Catholic Archbishop of Canterbury posted in all churches of the land a bull from the pope:

> ...wherein the Pope declares himself perfectly convinced of the guilt of the order, and solemnly denounces the penalty of excommunication against all persons, of whatever rank, station, or condition in life, whether clergy or laity, who should knowingly afford, either publicly or privately, assistance, counsel, or kindness to the Templars, or should dare to shelter them, or give them countenance or protection, and also laying under interdict all cities, castles, lands, and places, which should harbour any of the members of the proscribed order.[30]

This was a declaration of the Templars' guilt prior to their trial. That clear act did not show the pope as impartial, let alone reconciled with the Templar Order by the actions at Chinon. But there

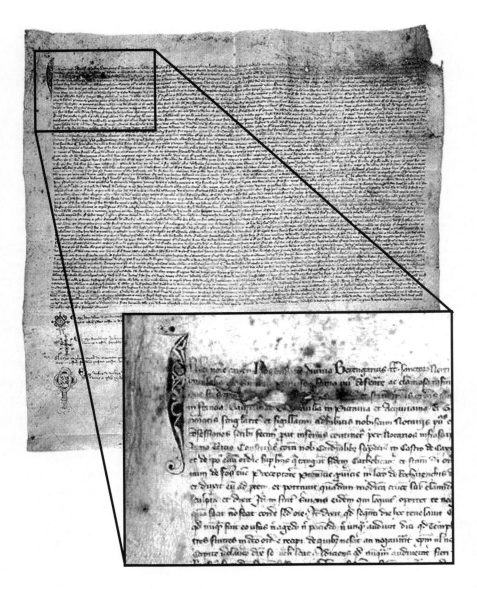

Fig. 36   Chinon Parchment

was more to come. During the next year the Templars in English prisons were questioned many times without obtaining proof of their guilt, so sterner measures were ordered.

> At first, king Edward the Second, to his honour, forbade the infliction of torture upon the illustrious members of the Temple in his dominions—men who had fought and bled for Christendom, and of whose piety and morals he had a short time before given such ample testimony to the principal sovereigns of Europe. But the virtuous resolution of the weak king was speedily overcome by the all-powerful influence of the Roman pontiff, who wrote to him in the month of June, upbraiding him for preventing the inquisitors from submitting the Templars to the discipline of the rack. Influenced by the admonitions of the pope, and the solicitations of the clergy, king Edward, on the 26th of August, sent orders to John de Crumbewell, constable of the Tower, to deliver up all the Templars in his custody, at the request of the inquisitors....[31]

In France at that same time a number of Templars who had previously confessed under duress now fully asserted their innocence. As we have seen, King Philip had fifty-four of these men brought before the archbishop at Sens, a city to the southeast of Paris, who passed judgment on those Templars on behalf of the Church.

> "...you have fallen into the sin of *heresy*. By your confession and repentance you had merited absolution, and had once more become reconciled to the church. As you have revoked your confession, the church no longer regards you as reconciled, but as having fallen back to your first errors. You are, therefore, *relapsed heretics* and as such, we condemn you to the fire." [32]

They were burned at the stake the following day. This revealed how fleeting the reconciliation with the Church was for those Templars.

At Chinon, the proceedings show Jacques de Molay and the other Templar leaders were not found innocent as some have suggested. They were required instead to falsely declare they were guilty of some form of heresy. The Church then pardoned them for their guilt, and pronounced them to have been reconciled. Even so, the pope then left de Molay and the others to languish in prison for six more years. On the 18th of March 1314, after another quick trial in front of three cardinals appointed by the Vatican, those Templar leaders were condemned to spend the rest of their life in prison. Having finally had more than he could bear—of giving "confessions" in hope of winning freedom for himself and his men, but never gaining that reward—Jacques de Molay stepped forward and loudly declared his innocence, and the innocence of his Order. One of the other Templar officers joined him in that affirmation. This declaration of their innocence made them "relapsed heretics."

> The same day at dusk they were led out of their dungeons, and were burned to death in a slow and lingering manner upon small fires of charcoal which were kindled on the little island in the Seine, between the king's garden and the convent of St. Augustine, close to the spot where now stands the equestrian statue of Henry IV.[33]

So the confessions obtained from these men at Chinon worked against them when they later pled their innocence. In what sense can it be said that the *Chinon Parchment* ever established the innocence of the Templars? How could it be claimed that *Chinon* relieved the Vatican of any guilt or embarrassment over the treatment of the Knights Templar? None of those things seem to have occurred.

And so it all comes back to Chevalier Ramsay's declaration of the Templars being linked to Masons. The raw nerve touched in Rome by that assertion indicated that all had not yet healed. If Ramsay's statement was without merit, it could easily have been ignored. The excessive response to these newly-emerged Masons—a response elevated all the way to papal bull and excommunication—showed the members of the Vatican took Ramsay's claim very seriously.

Yet even as the Vatican moved in the direction of suppression, large numbers of people in the North moved in the opposite direction. A wave of revival and emulation of these Templars began, and it attracted many new members to Masonry. Those knights of the red cross still stirred admiration and fascination hundreds of years after their disappearance, and the attraction was growing.

In America, the fascination with Templar knights would also become strong one day. But first there was another pressing concern. English taxes on the colonists were provoking complaints of "no taxation without representation" and a growing rebellion against the king's government was getting under way.

Chapter
Thirty-Two

George Washington

Winds of change in the American colonies were just beginning to stir when George Washington was twenty years old and first walked into the Masonic lodge in Fredericksburg, Virginia. He was soon accepted by the brothers and initiated into Masonry on the 4th of November 1752. This lodge was just across the river from his home in Fredericksburg, so he was able to participate regularly. By the following year young George was passed to Fellow Craft and then raised to the degree of Master Mason.

Shortly thereafter a frontier conflict broke out that would become known as the French and Indian War and it had a profound effect on his life. Answering the call of duty, Washington gladly served in the American military units fighting alongside British troops. There he learned the difficult military tradecraft in clashes along the frontier that extended from Virginia to Ohio. It also gave George a chance to be part of the popular Masonic lodges in British camps. In that environment he met British officers and men "on the level" like equals, and a degree of camaraderie naturally developed.

In 1758, having sown his wild oats, Washington resigned his commission as Colonel in charge of Virginia's militia regiment.

Fig. 37   George Washington attired as Master

He proposed to Martha Custis, made her Martha Washington, and then settled into a landowners life at Mount Vernon. This magnificent estate had come to George by inheritance and enabled him to grow in stature among colonial society while presiding over thousands of acres of rich farmland, forests and river frontage.

But trouble was brewing. To pay for costs from the French and Indian War, Britain decided to tax the colonists. This Stamp Act in 1765 lit the fuse of the American Revolution. Proclaiming "no taxation without representation," people in all thirteen colonies began to protest peacefully and sometimes not so peacefully. Washington by this time was not only a prosperous landowner but also a member of the Virginia legislature. He helped to stir these troubles by introducing a bill to ban the importing of goods from Great Britain.

A further tax on tea led to the Boston Tea Party in 1774. A number of colonists disguised as Mohawk Indians unloaded three shiploads of British tea into the harbor. The king and Parliament were not amused and retaliated with the Intolerable Acts. These closed the port of Boston, put Massachusetts under the rule of a British general, and added other laws deemed threatening by the colonies. In response George Washington and his fellow Virginians met with representatives of the other colonies in the First Continental Congress at Philadelphia. They strongly objected to those acts and petitioned King George III for redress of their grievances. But then military confrontations began.

A secretive communication network linked all the American colonies by this time, much like the coordination described in the Peasants' Revolt of 1381. Paul Revere was a key member of this network and, not too surprisingly, was a Mason along with Washington, Franklin and other influential colonists. Paul had entered the Lodge of St. Andrew in Boston during 1760 and served as its Master ten years later. When the British general in Massachusetts sent troops toward Concord and Lexington, Paul Revere made his famous midnight ride on the 18th of April 1775 to give warning to the rebels. With that the fighting began in earnest.

The Second Continental Congress anxiously assembled a month later in Philadelphia to deal with this crisis. John Hancock, another Mason, was chosen as president of the congress. John was one of the wealthiest men in the colonies through his shipping business, and used that leverage to help the rebel cause. He joined the Lodge of St. Andrew in Boston two years after Paul Revere, and together the men worked on many projects, including the Boston Tea Party. When Revere made his midnight ride and rallied the countryside, one of his goals was to reach Lexington and help Hancock escape along with Samuel Adams. One month later Hancock was chosen to lead the Continental Congress.

That congress quickly pulled together the militias of all the colonies and formed the Continental Army, choosing George Washington to be its commanding general. Clearly, many members of the Continental Congress were not Masons. But similar to what happened when the Royal Society was formed in England, Masons worked with non-Masons to accomplish their goals—and fairly noticeably managed to keep the key roles for themselves.

Ben Franklin had long been active trying to pull the colonies together, and in 1754 even published in his newspaper the drawing of a snake cut into pieces—with one segment for each colony—and the words "Join or Die." This reflected an old legend

Fig. 38   Benjamin Franklin's political cartoon in 1754

about a cut snake coming back to life if the pieces were re-joined before sunset. That was believed to be the first political cartoon ever published in America. In 1775 his American snake, now whole, reappeared with new words under it, "Don't Tread on Me." He was present at the Continental Congress when the Marine Corps was formed, and his "Don't Tread on Me" image was adopted as its popular symbol.

King George III clarified the confrontation by issuing his Proclamation of Rebellion against the colonists. The uproar stirred by the quiet Templar rebellion was now recognized by both sides. Members of the Continental Congress responded to the king on the 4th of July 1776 by signing the Declaration of Independence. America would now be free from the British king—if they could just win the war.

Fig. 39   Colonial Marine Corps symbol in 1775

I Do Solemnly Swear

George Washington surrounded himself with officers in his Continental Army that he could trust. As a result, almost 50 percent of the 73 generals who served under him during the war were Masons. Those men had all been raised with the traditions of the fugitive Templars, including the strong bond of brotherhood, coming to the aid of a brother in distress, religious tolerance and a strong desire for freedom from excessive force by king or church. It made his daunting task a little easier—having this ready supply of dedicated men. Since he had only ragtag militias to lead against well trained and armed British soldiers, Washington was also a Mason in distress, so no brother could refuse him.

Men even came from overseas to help him in his hour of need. Washington reached across to French brother Marquis de Lafayette to bring France's support to his cause. This he was able to do even though their countries had recently been at war against each other. Another Mason came to his aid from Germany—Baron Von Steuben. The baron brought with him the professional training needed to build a working army.

Washington suffered losses as well as victories in the back-and-forth fortunes of war, with the outcome ever in doubt. Even so, in the throes of combat, he showed the extent to which the Templar and Masonic obligations affected his life. This was what happened after one such battle.

> In the 46th regiment of the British army there was a traveling Lodge, holding its Warrant of Constitution under the jurisdiction of the Grand Lodge of Ireland. After an engagement between the American and British forces, in which the latter were defeated, the private chest of the Lodge, containing its jewels, furniture and implements, fell into the hands of the Americans. The captors reported the circumstances to General Washington, who at once ordered the chest to be returned to the Lodge and the regiment, under a guard of honor. "The surprise," says the historian of the event, himself an Englishman and a Mason, "the feeling of both officers and men may be imagined, when they perceived the flag of truce that announced this elegant compliment from their noble opponent, but still more noble brother. The guard of honor, with their music playing a sacred march [carried] the chest containing the Constitution and implements of the Craft borne aloft, like another ark of the covenant, equally by Englishmen and Americans, who lately engaged in the strife of war." [34]

Washington aided his brothers in distress without hesitation. In days gone by, this action might have been called chivalry. To him it was simply living up to an obligation.

In any event, the war went on until Washington's final victory at Yorktown in 1781. It then remained for Franklin and others to negotiate the treaty that ended hostilities two years later.

That was all well and good, but now Washington, Franklin, Hancock and the others had to build a nation or they could lose their newly won freedom. To that end a Constitutional Convention was convened in Philadelphia during 1787, and George Washington was elected to preside over the drafting of the Constitution.

*Fig. 40   Washington presides over Constitutional Convention
with Franklin sitting at left*

That actually was a very strange thing to do in those days. There was no such thing as nations being ruled by constitutions. They were primarily ruled by kings and queens who made grants of rights to lords and commoners. Even in England, as advanced as it was, that system of rule was used. Masonic lodges and Grand Lodges had constitutions, but other than that it was a rare concept. After the Declaration of Independence, this Masonic practice became popular in the colonies. Now, with nothing else at hand, Washington and the others reached for something familiar to them—the writing of a constitution.

They did their job well, and the United States Constitution was officially ratified in 1788. But in the struggle to produce that document they had been unable to include guarantees of basic freedoms. When the ratification was completed, they immediately pressed for an American Bill of Rights. These were soon added as the first ten amendments to the Constitution.

Of course the first of these rights was that the government would make no law establishing an official religion for the country. That had been the constant goal of the fugitive Templars crushed by the Vatican. And it was practiced during all the years since then by Masons who acknowledged their belief in God but allowed each brother to worship according to his conscience.

Several amendments guaranteed fair trials, due process of law, and the requirement that people could not be forced to testify against themselves. The Inquisition had tortured and condemned the Templars without due process, and showed the importance of these things. They were now guaranteed.

It had been almost five hundred years since the knights in white were suddenly attacked by king and church in 1307. But the quiet rebellion against abusive power had been kept alive. Now George Washington, Benjamin Franklin and the other members of the long-standing rebellion had done their duty. The United States of America was created with no king and no fixed religious denomination. The excessive use of force by king or church was no longer possible.

In late April of 1789 George Washington arrived in New York City for his inauguration and was welcomed by enthusiastic crowds.

Fig. 41 George Washington takes the oath of office

On the appointed day for his swearing-in ceremony—April 30—he made his way to Federal Hall, went up to the second floor, and stepped out onto a broad balcony. There he placed his hand on a Masonic Bible.

It was a Bible like the one you might buy in any bookstore, but it resided in St. John's Lodge No. 1 in New York City. Its significance to Washington was that countless Masons had placed their hand on this Bible when they took their obligations. He had done the same as a young man many years earlier, and now he was taking an equally serious obligation to serve his country. Those were things he held as important in his life.

Sir Walter de Clifton and his fellow Templars had taken their obligations to the Order with their hands on a Bible. And after the inferno, as fugitives, they took oaths to stand by their surviving brothers—which became the Masonic obligations. Those oaths and obligations were undiminished by the years, being passed hand-to-hand and mouth-to-ear in a way that still reached brothers as strongly as Washington had been reached. Most Masons met those obligations quietly. Washington met his obligations clearly and publicly.

With his hand on that Bible, he took the oath of office. And he became the first President of the United States.

Additional details and source materials are
seen in *Sworn in Secret* by Sanford Holst

Phoenician Secrets further explores the rich society
of great sea traders in the ancient Mediterranean

*Fig. 42   Seated beside the Apprentice Pillar in Rosslyn Chapel
a man looks down the stairs to the Lower Chapel*

Sir Walter at Rosslyn

When the Templar trials at Edinburgh ended in 1309, Sir Walter de Clifton was surprised to be set free. Not wanting to risk his good fortune further, he quickly returned to Balantrodoch—the main Templar estate in Scotland—packed his few belongings, and set out to find his brothers who disappeared before his trial. They had not told him where they were going, so that their whereabouts could not be extracted from him by torture. But he knew where they would come to look for him.

Given the strict secrecy involved, following Walter's steps was difficult. Fortunately a trail of clues was left behind in public and private records to show what happened at Rosslyn Chapel. And it only added to the mystique surrounding that intriguing church.

When Henry St. Clair, the 3rd Baron of Roslin, began to build a castle for his family around 1205 AD, he chose to put it on the spot where Rosslyn Chapel would one day stand.[35] The land upon which this stone-block manor was built sloped downward to the east, and it was in this lower part of the residence that the family chapel was built. For the next one hundred years, the St. Clair barons were able to ride to dinner at the neighboring Templar manor in only thirty minutes' time, and the Templars could do the same.

In 1307, when John de Hueflete and the other Templars hastily departed from Balantrodoch, the closest and safest place for them to take shelter was this chapel in the St. Clair manor. The Baron of Roslin could not shelter them openly due to the sentence of ex-communication proclaimed by the pope upon all who aided the Templars, but he was entirely capable of doing it privately. In fact the St. Clair family had a long history of sheltering people who were stung by the power of church or state. That was shown when they permitted outlawed gypsies to live on the grounds until rep-resentatives of the king protested loudly enough that the Baron of Roslin was forced to desist.[36] The St. Clairs were not only capable of harboring the fugitive Templars, but had a history of enjoying the performance of that act.

This chapel at the lower part of the St. Clair estate had two out-side doors which allowed access directly from the surrounding hillside. That meant visitors to the chapel could avoid using the main entrance to the manor employed by the family. Individuals could come and go quietly at night without being observed. Of course any fugitives who took refuge there would move on to permanent housing when it could be arranged.

Yet after they moved on the problem of having private meet-ings in their permanent housing was still a concern, with neigh-bors watching. Fortunately this private chapel on the St. Clair es-tate was still available as a meeting place, surrounded by the soli-tude of the baron's property. A fugitive Templar such as Sir Wal-ter need only hide there until the next meeting of his brothers, and he would be together with them again.

One indication that this is what happened was shown in what followed. In 1441 — when the St. Clairs had already built a larger and more secure castle nearby — they began to tear down their old manor house. They removed all of the manor except for the small chapel. For some reason that single room was preserved exactly as it stood, even though its location interfered with the majestic de-sign of Rosslyn Chapel being built above it. Were the early St. Clair lords and ladies buried here? No, there was a separate out-door graveyard for them, and the future lords and ladies were buried in the main crypt of Rosslyn Chapel, not this ancient Lower Chapel, as it is called. Yet some strangely emotional reason existed for preserving this modest stone chapel—because we can still walk into the magnificently ornate Rosslyn Chapel today and descend those rustic stairs to the Lower Chapel below.

Fig. 43 The Lower Chapel

By all indications, this was one of the first asylums for the fugitive Templars, and continued to be the hall in which those men met when they began to call themselves Masons in the 1300s. The lords of the hall in which they met almost certainly had to be initiated into this group that gathered in their chapel. After more than a hundred and thirty years of lodge meetings in this place—from 1307 to 1441—it would clearly be understandable for the lord of Roslin to order that this chapel be retained.

If in fact this is what happened, then the Lower Chapel is one of the first Masonic lodge rooms that came into existence after 1307. That would make it the oldest such room that has not been torn down and can still be seen today.

Fig. 44 Antiquities of the Temple in London

Condemnation

Not all of the condemnation of Masonry by the Vatican was based upon this secretive organization's connection with Knights Templar. In 1884 Pope Leo XIII listed specific allegations of which Masonry was accused in his formal letter *Humanum genus*. It is a surprising list.

Freemasons were condemned for supporting the election of government leaders by the people. They were further condemned for advocating the separation of church and state. And Masons were condemned for allowing the education of children by teachers who were not members of the Catholic Church.

If that sounds incredible, consider this official transcript of his words released by the Vatican.

> Therefore, in the education and instruction of children they allow no share, either of teaching or of discipline, to the ministers of the Church; and in many places they have procured that the education of youth shall be exclusively in the hands of laymen, and that nothing which treats of the most important and most holy

duties of men to God shall be introduced into the instructions on morals.

Then come their doctrines of politics, in which the naturalists lay down that all men have the same right, and are in every respect of equal and like condition; that each one is naturally free; that no one has the right to command another; that it is an act of violence to require men to obey any authority other than that which is obtained from themselves. According to this, therefore, all things belong to the free people; power is held by the command or permission of the people, so that, when the popular will changes, rulers may lawfully be deposed and the source of all rights and civil duties is either in the multitude or in the governing authority when this is constituted according to the latest doctrines. It is held also that the State should be without God; that in the various forms of religion there is no reason why one should have precedence of another; and that they are all to occupy the same place.

That these doctrines are equally acceptable to the Freemasons, and that they would wish to constitute States according to this example and model, is too well known to require proof. For some time past they have openly endeavoured to bring this about with all their strength and resources.

So Masons were accused of supporting democracy and freedom of religion. Based on the work of George Washington, Ben Franklin and many others, it is fair to say that accusation is correct. Does that make them worthy of condemnation? Probably not.

Even though the Vatican's attacks on Templars and Masons seem to have been made for less than desirable reasons, that made no difference. The condemnations were repeated by people of many denominations who were not really clear what the accused people might have done.

On the other hand, it must reasonably be said that Templars and Masons contributed to their own problems to some degree by being secretive and not disclosing what they were doing.

In any event, the Templars' long narrative is now an open book. Their story is as old as Solomon's Temple, as bright as a Templar sword, and as personal as a president's oath of office.

Fig. 45   The Templar church at Balantrodoch in Scotland still stands today

Illustrations

Front cover — Templar medallion graphic (by Sanford Holst)
Back cover — Battle of Montgisard (by Charles-Philippe Larivière)

Figure

Figure

Figure

Annotations

[1] *Reg. Clem. V*, year 6, nos. 7527-7528, p. 439; also Barber, Malcolm, *The Trial of the Templars*. (Cambridge: Cambridge University Press, 1978/2006), p. 248.

[2] 2 Samuel 5:11

[3] Strabo, *Geography* 3:5:11.

[4] Robinson, John J. *Born In Blood: The Lost Secrets of Freemasonry*. (New York: Evans & Co, 1989), p.72.

[5] This account was based on a journal attributed to Geoffrey de Vinsauf, who was said to have accompanied King Richard on his Crusade, as well as the writings of Jacques de Vitry and others. It was documented in Addison, *The History of the Knights Templars*. (London: Longman, Brown, Green &Longmans, 1842), pp. 141-49.

[6] *Histoire de Languedoc*, lib. xvii, p. 407; *Hist. de l'eglise de Gandersheim*; *Mariana de rebus Hispaniae*, lib. x. cap. 15, 17, 18.; *Zurita anales de la corona de Aragon*, tom. i, lib. i. cap. 52; and *Quarita*, tom. i, lib. ii. cap.4; also Addison, *The History of the Knights Templars*, pp. 28-29.

[7] Templar of Tyre, *Cronaca del Templare di Tiro (1243-1314): la caduta degli Stati Crociati nel racconto di un testimone oculare*, edited and translated by L. Minervini (Naples: 2000), para.262, pp. 216-19; *The 'Templar of Tyre'. Part III of the 'Deeds of the Cypriots'*, translated by P. Crawford (Aldershot: 2003), para. 498, pp. 111-13. The translation has been anglicised; also Barber, Malcolm, *The Trial of the Templars*, pp. 5-6.

[8] De excidio urbis Acconis apud *Martene*, tom. v. col. 757. *De Guignes*, Hist. des Huns, tom. iv. p. 162. *Michaud*, Extraits Arabes, p. 762, 808. Abulfarag. Chron. Syr. p. 595. Wilkens, Comment. Abulfed. Hist. p. 231-234. *Marin. Sanut Torsell*, lib. iii. pars 12, cap. 21; also Addison, *The History of the Knights Templars*, pp. 186-192.

[9] Matthew of Paris *Chronica Majora*, vol. iv, p. 641; vol. vi, pi42. See Bulst-Thiele *Magistri*, p. 254, n.87; also Barber, *The New Knighthood*, pp. 199-200.

[10] Addison, *The History of the Knights Templars*, pp. 204-205.

[11] Barber, *The Trial of the Templars*, pp. 279-80.

[12] Barber, *The Trial of the Templars*, pp. 218-219.

[13] Thornbury, Walter and Edward Walford. *Old and New London: A Narrative of Its History, Its People and Its Places: The Southern Suburbs*. (London: Cassell & Company, 1893), Vol. VI, pp. 76-77.

[14] Addison, Charles G. *The History of the Knights Templars*, pp. 226-229.

[15] Addison, *The History of the Knights Templars*, p. 240.

[16] *Reg. Clem. V*, year 6, nos. 7527-7528, p. 439; also Barber, Malcolm, *The Trial of the Templars*, p. 248.

[17] Barber, Malcolm, *The Trial of the Templars*, p. 250.

[18] Addison, *The History of the Knights Templars*, pp. 279-280.

[19] Bulloch, *Scottish Notes and Queries*, Vol. IV, issue 6 (December 1902), p. 83.

[20] Barbour, John. *The Bruce: Being the Metrical History of Robert the Bruce, King of Scots, Compiled A.D. 1375*, translated by George Eyre-Todd (London: Gowans & Gray Ltd, 1907), p. 194-224.

[21] Scott, Sir Walter. *Lay of the Last Minstrel*. (New York: C.S. Francis & Co., 1845), Canto Sixth, XXIII, pp. 178-179.

[22] Carr, *Grand Lodge 1717-1967*. (Oxford: United Grand Lodge of England, 1967), p. 38.

[23] Churchill, Winston *A History of the English-Speaking Peoples* (London: Cassell, 1956), vol. 1.

[24] Robinson, *Born in Blood*, pp. 57-58.

[25] Robinson, *Born in Blood*, pp. 30-31.

[26] Robertson, *The life of Sir Robert Moray: soldier, statesman and man of science (1608-1673)*. (London: Longmans, Green & Co., 1922), p. 1.

[27] Hearne, Thomas *Peter Langtoft's Chronicle* (Oxford, 1725), Vol. I, pp. 161-164. (Reprinted in London by Samuel Bagster in a collection titled *The Works of Thomas Hearne, Volume III*).

[28] Plot, Robert *Natural History of Staffordshire* (Oxford: Theatre, 1686), p. 316.

[29] Cooper, *The Rosslyn Hoax?* (Hersham, Surrey: Lewis Masonic, 2007), p. 351.

[30] *Processus contra Templarios* by W. Dugdale in *Monasticon Anglicanum* (1830) Vol. VI, part 2, pp. 844-46; also Addison, *The History of the Knights Templars*, p. 214.

[31] Arch. secret. Vatican. Registr. literar. curiae anno 5 domini Clementis Papae 5.—Raynouard, p. 152. And Acta Rymeri, tom. iii. ad ann. 1310, p. 224; also Addison, *The History of the Knights Templars*, pp. 242-43.

[32] Joan. can. Sanct. Vict. Contin. de Nangis ad ann. 1310. Ex secundâ vitâ *Clem*. V. p. 37; also Addison, *The History of the Knights Templars*, p. 240.

[33] Addison, *The History of the Knights Templars*, pp. 279-280.

34 Mackey, Albert G. *Washington as a Freemason: An Address Delivered before the Grand and Subordinate Lodges of Ancient Freemasons of South Carolina, at Charleston, S.C., on Thursday, November 4th, 1852, being the Centennial Celebration of the Initiation of George Washington.* (Charleston: Miller, 1852).

35 While we examined Rosslyn Chapel in 2008, the Rosslyn Trust staff gave me the dates of construction for the original St. Clair manor as 1205-1210.

36 Cooper, *The Rosslyn Hoax*, pp. 118-120.

Bibliography

Addison, Charles G. *The History of the Knights Templars*. London: Longman, Brown, Green & Longmans, 1842.

_____ and Robert Macoy *The Knights Templar History*. New York: Masonic Publishing, 1874/1912.

Anderson, James. *The Constitutions of the Free-Masons*. Philadelphia: Benjamin Franklin, 1734.

_____ *New Book of Constitutions*. London: Grand Lodge of England, 1738.

Anderson, William. *The Scottish Nation*. Edinburgh: A. Fullarton & Co., 1877.

Baigent, Michael, Richard Leigh and Henry Lincoln. *Holy Blood, Holy Grail*. New York: Delacorte Press, 1982.

Baigent, Michael and Richard Leigh. *The Temple and the Lodge*. New York: Arcade, 1989.

Barber, Malcolm. *The Trial of the Templars*. Cambridge: Cambridge University Press, First edition 1978, Second edition 2006.

_____ *The New Knighthood: A History of the Order of the Temple*. Cambridge: Cambridge University Press, 1994.

Barbour, John. *The Bruce: Being the Metrical History of Robert the Bruce, King of Scots, Compiled A.D. 1375.* (translated by George Eyre-Todd) London: Gowans & Gray Ltd, 1907.

Baynes, Thomas Spencer, editor. *Encyclopaedia Britannica.* New York: Henry G. Allen, 1888.

Bernard of Clairvaux. *Epistolae,* in *Sancti Bernardi Opera.* (ed. J. Leclercq and H. Rochais) Rome: Editiones Cistercienses, 1974.

Bikai, Patricia *The Pottery of Tyre.* Warminster, UK: Aris & Phillips, 1978.

Boardman, John et al, eds. *The Oxford History of the Roman World.* Oxford: Oxford University Press, 1986.

Bulloch, John. *Scottish Notes and Queries.* Aberdeen: A. Brown & Co, 1903.

Burgoyne, Michael Hamilton. "1187 – 1260" in *Where Heaven and Earth Meet: Jerusalem's Sacred Esplanade.* (ed. Oleg Grabar and Benjamin Z. Kedar) Austin: University of Texas Press, 2009.

Burnes, James. *Sketch of the History of the Knights Templars.* Edinburgh: William Blackwood & Sons, 1840.

Cancik, Hubert and Helmuth Schneider, eds. *Brill's New Pauly Encyclopedia of the Ancient World.* Leiden, The Netherlands: Brill, 2002.

Carr, Harry. *The Minutes of the Lodge of Edinburgh, Mary's Chapel, No. 1 (1598-1738).* London: Quatuor Coronati Lodge, 1962.

_____ "Freemasonry Before Grand Lodge" *Grand Lodge 1717-1967.* Oxford: United Grand Lodge of England, 1967.

Casson, Lionel. *The Ancient Mariners.* Princeton, New Jersey: Princeton University Press, 1991.

_____ *Ships and Seamanship in the Ancient World.* Baltimore, Maryland: John Hopkins University Press, 1995.

Cooper, Robert L.D. *Cracking the Freemasons Code.* New York: Atria Books, 2006.

_____ *The Rosslyn Hoax?* Hersham, Surrey: Lewis Masonic, 2007.

Churchill, Winston *A History of the English-Speaking Peoples.* London: Cassell, 1956.

Davies, Vivian and Renee Friedman. *Egypt Uncovered.* New York: Stewart, Tabori & Chang, 1998.

Dueck, Daniela. *Strabo of Amasia.* London: Routledge, 2000.

Dunand, Maurice. *Byblos.* (French, translated into English by H. Tabet.) Paris: Librairie Adrien-Maisonneuve, 1973.

Friedman, Renee. "The Ceremonial Centre at Hierakonpolis, Locality HK29A" *Aspects of Early Egypt.* (ed. A.J. Spencer) London: British Museum Press, 1996.

Gould, R.F. with D. Wright editor. *Gould's History of Freemasonry.* London: Caxton Publishing, 1931.

Grant, Michael. *The Ancient Mediterranean.* New York: Charles Scribner's Sons, 1969.

Haag, Michael. *The Templars: The History & the Myth.* New York: Harper, 2009.

Haunch, T.O. "The Formation-Part 1, 1717-1751" in *Grand Lodge 1717-1967.* Oxford: United Grand Lodge of England, 1967.

Hay, Richard Augustine. *Genealogie of the Saintclaires of Rosslyn.* Edinburgh: Thomas G. Stevenson, 1835.

Hearne, Thomas *Peter Langtoft's Chronicle* (Oxford, 1725), Vol. I, pp. 161-164. (Reprinted in London by Samuel Bagster in a collection titled *The Works of Thomas Hearne, Volume III*).

Herodotus. *The History.* (Greek, translated into English by George Rawlinson.) New York: Tandy Thomas Co., 1909.

Holst, Sanford. *Phoenician Secrets: Exploring the Ancient Mediterrranean.* Los Angeles: Santorini Publishing, 2011.

_____ *Sworn in Secret: Freemasonry and the Knights Templar.* Los Angeles: Santorini Publishing, 2012.

Josten, C. H. ed. *Elias Ashmole (1617–1692). His Autobiographical and Historical Notes, his Correspondence, and Other Contemporary Sources Relating to his Life and Work.* Oxford: Clarendon Press, 1966.

Knight, Christopher and Robert Lomas. *The Hiram Key*. Gloucester, MA: Fair Winds Press, 1996.

Lagassé, Paul et al, eds. *The Columbia Encyclopedia, Sixth Edition*. New York: Columbia University Press, 2001-04.

Lomas, Robert. *The Invisible College*. London: Headline Publishing, 2002.

_____ *Turning the Templar Key*. Beverly, MA: Fair Winds Press, 2007.

Mackey, Albert G. *Washington as a Freemason: An Address Delivered before the Grand and Subordinate Lodges of Ancient Freemasons of South Crolina, at Charleston, S.C., on Thursday, November 4th, 1852, being the Centennial Celebration of the Initiation of George Washington*. Charleston: Miller, 1852.

_____ *Encyclopedia of Freemasonry*. London: Griffin, 1870.

_____ *The History of Freemasonry*. New York: Masonic History Co, 1898.

Manuel des Chevaliers de l'Ordre du Temple. Paris: Chevaliers de l'Ordre du Temple, 1825.

Markoe, Glenn E. *Phoenicians: Peoples of the Past*. Berkeley: University of California Press, 2000.

Meyers, Eric, ed. *Oxford Encyclopedia of Archaeology in the Near East*. New York: Oxford University Press, 1997.

Moscati, Sabatino, ed. *The Phoenicians*. New York: Rizzoli International, 1999.

N/A. *The Holy Bible, King James Version*. 1987.

Plot, Robert. *Natural History of Staffordshire*. Oxford: Theatre, 1686.

Redford, Donald, ed. *The Oxford Encyclopedia of Ancient Egypt*. New York: Oxford University Press, 2001.

Ritmeyer, Leen. *The Quest: Revealing the Temple Mount in Jerusalem*. Jerusalem: Carta, 2006.

Robertson, Alexander. *The life of Sir Robert Moray: soldier, statesman and man of science (1608-1673)*. London: Longmans, Green & Co., 1922.

Robinson, John J. *Born In Blood: The Lost Secrets of Freemasonry*. New York: M. Evans, 1989.

——————— *A Pilgrim's Path*. New York: M. Evans, 1993.

Sasson, Jack M., ed. *Civilizations of the Ancient Near East*. New York: Charles Scribner's Sons, 1995.

Scott, Sir Walter. *Lay of the Last Minstrel*. New York: C.S. Francis & Co., 1845.

Stevenson, David. *The Origins of Freemasonry*. Cambridge: Cambridge University Press, 1988/2005.

Statutes of the Religious and Military Order of the Temple, as Established in Scotland; with an Historical Notice of the Order. Edinburgh: Grand Conclave, 1843.

Thornbury, Walter and Edward Walford. *Old and New London: A Narrative of Its History, Its People and Its Places: The Southern Suburbs*. London: Cassell & Company, 1893.

Walbank, F.W. ed. *Cambridge Ancient History*. Cambridge: Cambridge University Press, 1989.

Ward, J.S.M. *Freemasonry and the Ancient Gods*. London: Simpkin, Marshall, Hamilton, Kent & Co., 1921.

Weld, Charles Richard. *A History of the Royal Society, with Memoirs of the Presidents*. London: John W. Parker, 1848.

Williams, Louis. "Sir Christopher Wren" in *Fiat Lux*. Sebring, Ohio: Philalethes Society, 2009.

Index

W

Walter de Clifton. *See* Clifton,
Walter de
Washington, George, 198-208,
217, 222, 230
Westminster, 164-165, 179, 182
Wilkins, John, 169, 170, 176
William the Conqueror, 90,
121

Winding Staircase, 134, 139
Wren, Christopher, 167, 171-
173, 231
Wycliffe, John, 154-155

Y

York, 79, 134, 179, 183

3809639R00138

Printed in Great Britain
by Amazon.co.uk, Ltd.,
Marston Gate.